T3-BEA-157

TRIM THE FAT

WITH

CHEESES

PUBLICATIONS INTERNATIONAL, LTD.

Copyright © 1996 by Publications International, Ltd.
Recipes and text copyright © 1996 Alpine Lace Brands.
All rights reserved. This publication may not be reproduced or quoted in whole or in part by any means whatsoever without written permission from Louis Weber, C.E.O. Permission is never granted for commercial purposes.

ALPINE LACE is a registered trademark of Alpine Lace Brands, Inc., Maplewood, NJ 07040.

This edition published by Publications International, Ltd., 7373 N. Cicero Ave., Lincolnwood, IL 60646.

Recipes developed by Alpine Lace Brands, Inc. and Beth Allen Associates, Inc.

Photography: Sacco Productions Limited, Chicago

Pictured on the front cover: Chicken Enchiladas *(page 48)*.

Pictured on the back cover *(from top to bottom):* Chicken Sesame with Oriental Crème *(page 8),* Butterflied Shrimp Parmesan *(page 44)* and Napoleons *(page 92).*

ISBN: 0-7853-1964-6

Manufactured in U.S.A.

8 7 6 5 4 3 2 1

Nutritional Analysis: Nutritional information is given for the recipes in this publication. Each analysis is based on the food items in the ingredient list, except ingredients labeled as "optional." When more than one ingredient choice is listed, the first ingredient is used for analysis. If a range for the amount of the ingredient is given, nutritional analysis is based on the lowest amount. Foods offered as "serve with" suggestions are not included in the analysis unless otherwise stated. Recipes were developed within the dietary guidelines of the American Heart Association.

TRIM THE FAT
WITH

CHEESES

COOKING THE Alpine Lace WAY

Cooking and eating in moderation makes good healthy sense. It's simple when you begin with Alpine Lace® cheeses. Slice them, dice them, shred them or melt them. Toss them into salads, layer them in sandwiches or sprinkle them on top of casseroles. Stuff them into chicken, bake them in breads or add them to desserts—they all taste terrific! Use them as much as you like in place of full fat, full sodium cheeses! Alpine Lace® offers an ever-expanding line of great-tasting cheese products—fat free, reduced fat and reduced sodium. As a company, we strive to produce the greatest quality products that are always nutritionally superior to their regular cheese counterparts. We've even added boneless cooked ham to our product line—each one-ounce slice has only one gram of fat. Bite after bite, recipe after recipe, you'll never miss the extra calories or fat, for we've left in the great taste!

FAT FACTS!

Registered dietitians and organizations, such as the American Heart Association, recommend that 30% or less of total daily calories comes from fat. This cookbook was developed within these guidelines. The flag at the top of each recipe tells you at a glance the real fat facts:

■ Fat Free—Each serving has less than a half a gram of fat.

■ Low Fat—30% or less of calories in each serving comes from fat.

■ Reduced Fat—Each serving has less fat than the traditional recipe (shown as a percentage).

NUTRITIONAL COMPARISONS

The nutrition chart at the end of each recipe compares the Alpine Lace® recipe with its traditional recipe in calories, calories from fat, total fat and cholesterol. The Alpine Lace® recipes use health-wise ingredients as listed in the left column of the chart on page 7. The traditional recipes used for nutritional comparison include ingredients from the right column. By substituting healthful ingredients into your everyday cooking and eating, you'll soon be on your way to a healthier lifestyle.

Alpine Lace® Recipe	Traditional Recipe
Dairy: Low fat milk, buttermilk, part-skim ricotta, fat free sour cream, butter substitute	Whole milk, whole-milk ricotta, regular sour cream, cream, butter
Cheeses: Alpine Lace® fat free, reduced fat or reduced sodium cheeses	Full fat and/or full sodium cheeses
Egg substitute	Fresh eggs
Reduced fat mayonnaise and nonfat mayonnaise dressing	Regular mayonnaise
Canned products: No-salt-added tomato paste and tomato juice	Regular canned products
Low sodium broths and stocks: fat skimmed off	Regular broths and stocks: fat not skimmed off
Poultry without skin	Poultry with skin
Chops and roasts: well trimmed of fat	Meats without extra trimming
Ground beef round	Ground beef
Ham: Alpine Lace® 97% fat free/45% less sodium than regular ham	Untrimmed, regular boneless, cooked cured ham
Oven frying with no extra oil	Top-of-the-range frying in oil
Nonstick skillets and nonstick sprays	Regular skillets and oil
Optional ingredients excluded	Optional ingredients included

COOKING WITH LOW FAT CHEESES

Since most Alpine Lace® cheeses are fat free or reduced in fat, they take a little special handling and know-how when cooking with them. Here are some hints to assure terrific results.

■ When making a cream cheese sauce, first bring the liquid to a boil. Then add the fat free cream cheese and stir constantly until melted.

■ Bake casseroles completely and sprinkle with shredded cheese when they come out of the oven. The heat from the food melts the cheese.

■ When broiling with reduced fat cheeses, add the cheeses during the last 3 minutes.

■ To make cheeseburgers, add the cheese after the burgers are cooked. The hot burgers melt the cheese.

■ When adding cheese to soups and stews, stir in during the last 5 minutes of cooking.

■ When baking layered dishes, such as lasagna, cover with foil before baking.

APPETIZERS & SNACKS

It's party time—and Alpine Lace® comes to the rescue!
Choose from quick-to-mix dips, easy quesadillas,
delicious bruschetta—and many more. By starting with
appetizers featuring reduced fat or fat free cheeses, you're
sure to kick off the party in a healthy, great-tasting way.

LOW FAT

CHICKEN SESAME WITH ORIENTAL CRÈME

⅓ cup reduced sodium soy sauce
2 teaspoons minced garlic
1 teaspoon dark sesame oil
½ teaspoon ground ginger
1 pound boneless, skinless
    chicken breasts, cut into
    4 × ½-inch strips
6 ounces (1 carton) Alpine
    Lace® Fat Free Cream
    Cheese with Garlic & Herbs

2 tablespoons finely chopped
    green onions
2 tablespoons sesame seeds,
    toasted
1 tablespoon extra virgin
    olive oil

1 To marinate the chicken: In a small bowl, whisk the soy sauce, garlic, sesame oil and ginger. Reserve 2 tablespoons and pour the remaining marinade into a self-sealing plastic bag. Add the chicken pieces and seal the bag. Turn the bag to coat all the chicken, then refrigerate for at least 2 hours, turning the bag occasionally.

2 To make the Oriental Crème: In another small bowl, place the cream cheese. Whisk in the reserved 2 tablespoons of marinade and stir in the green onions. Cover with plastic wrap and refrigerate.

continued on page 10

Chicken party bites the Oriental way—high in flavor and low in fat!

3 To prepare the chicken: Remove the chicken from the marinade and discard any remaining marinade. Spread the sesame seeds on a plate and roll the chicken strips in them until lightly coated.

4 In a large nonstick skillet, heat the olive oil over medium-high heat. Add the chicken and stir-fry for 6 minutes or until golden brown and the juices run clear when the chicken is pierced with a fork. Serve with the Oriental Crème.
Makes 24 appetizer servings

Nutritional Comparison Per Serving
(1 appetizer serving)

Alpine Lace® Recipe		Traditional Recipe	
Calories	43	Calories	63
Calories from Fat	13	Calories from Fat	43
Total Fat	1 g	Total Fat	5 g
Cholesterol	13 mg	Cholesterol	17 mg

LOW FAT

QUESADILLAS

4 flour tortillas (8-inch)
¾ cup (3 ounces) shredded Alpine Lace® American Flavor Pasteurized Process Cheese Product with Jalapeño Peppers, divided
⅓ cup finely chopped green onions, divided

2 tablespoons minced fresh cilantro or ¼ cup minced fresh parsley, divided
1 small avocado, peeled, seeded and thinly sliced lengthwise (optional)
½ cup chunky salsa

1 Preheat the oven to 350°F. Arrange 2 tortillas on a baking sheet. Top each tortilla with half the cheese, half the green onions and half the cilantro. Cover each with a second tortilla, pressing down lightly with your hands.

2 Bake for 10 minutes or until the cheese melts and the tortillas are crisp. Cut each quesadilla into 6 wedges. Garnish each wedge with a slice of avocado, if you wish, and a spoonful of salsa.
Makes 12 appetizer servings

Nutritional Comparison Per Serving
(1 wedge)

Alpine Lace® Recipe		Traditional Recipe	
Calories	59	Calories	65
Calories from Fat	18	Calories from Fat	25
Total Fat	2 g	Total Fat	3 g
Cholesterol	5 mg	Cholesterol	7 mg

REDUCED FAT

40% less fat than the traditional recipe

CHEDDAR WAFERS

1½ cups (6 ounces) shredded Alpine Lace® Fat Free Pasteurized Process Skim Milk Cheese Product— For Cheddar Lovers
¼ cup butter, softened
3 tablespoons vegetable oil

1¼ cups unsifted all-purpose flour
½ teaspoon salt
½ teaspoon dry mustard
¼ teaspoon cayenne pepper
Paprika

1 In the bowl of a food processor, process the cheese and butter for about 30 seconds or until combined. With the machine running, slowly pour the oil through the feed tube.

2 Add the flour, salt, mustard and pepper. Process for 30 seconds or just until the mixture resembles coarse crumbs. (*Avoid overprocessing!*) Remove the dough, shape into a ball, wrap in plastic wrap and refrigerate for 30 minutes.

3 Preheat the oven to 350°F. Shape the dough into ¾-inch balls and place them 2 inches apart on 2 baking sheets. (You will have about 30 balls.)

4 Using the tines of a fork, slightly flatten each ball in a crisscross pattern until it resembles a ⅛-inch-thick coin.

5 Bake for 15 minutes or just until crisp, but not browned. Transfer wafers to wire racks, dust lightly with paprika and cool. Store in an airtight container.

Makes 2½ dozen wafers

Nutritional Comparison Per Serving
(1 wafer)

Alpine Lace® Recipe		Traditional Recipe	
Calories	55	Calories	68
Calories from Fat	28	Calories from Fat	44
Total Fat	3 g	Total Fat	5 g
Cholesterol	5 mg	Cholesterol	10 mg

REDUCED FAT

50% less fat than the traditional recipe

POTATO SKINS WITH CHEDDAR MELT

4 medium-size Idaho baking
   potatoes (about 2 pounds)
4 slices lean turkey bacon
2 tablespoons vegetable oil
2 cups (8 ounces) shredded
   Alpine Lace® Reduced Fat
   Cheddar Cheese

¼ cup fat free sour cream
2 tablespoons finely chopped
   chives or green onions
1 tablespoon minced jalapeño
   pepper

1 Place a piece of foil on the bottom rack of the oven and preheat the oven to 425°F. Scrub the potatoes well and pierce the skins a few times with a sharp knife. Place the potatoes directly on the middle oven rack and bake for 1 hour or until soft.

2 Meanwhile, in a small skillet, cook the bacon over medium heat until crisp. Drain on paper towels, then crumble the bacon.

3 Using a serrated knife, cut the potatoes in half lengthwise. With a small spoon, scoop out the pulp, leaving a ¼-inch-thick shell. (Save the potato pulp for another use.) Cut the skins into appetizer-size triangles.

4 Place the skins on a baking sheet, brush the insides with the oil and bake for 15 minutes or until crisp.

5 Remove the skins from the oven, sprinkle with the cheese and return to the oven for 5 minutes or until the cheese melts. Top the skins with the sour cream, then sprinkle with the chives, jalapeño pepper and bacon.

Makes about 24 appetizers

Nutritional Comparison Per Serving
(1 appetizer)

Alpine Lace® Recipe		Traditional Recipe	
Calories	58	Calories	79
Calories from Fat	28	Calories from Fat	53
Total Fat	3 g	Total Fat	6 g
Cholesterol	7 mg	Cholesterol	13 mg

Potato skins topped with melted reduced fat Cheddar—
a forever favorite that's skimmed down in fat,
yet still has that old-fashioned flavor.

CRUDITÉS WITH CREAMY CHEESE DIP

CREAMY CHEESE DIP

12 ounces (2 cartons) Alpine Lace® Fat Free Cream Cheese with Garlic & Herbs

⅔ cup nonfat mayonnaise dressing

⅓ cup finely chopped red onion

1 tablespoon whole-grain Dijon mustard

½ teaspoon freshly ground black pepper

¼ teaspoon curry powder

Red onion rings (optional)

CRUDITÉS

Assorted fresh vegetables (your choices!): bell pepper strips (green, red and yellow), broccoli florets, peeled baby carrots, celery sticks, whole green beans,

mushroom slices, snow peas, yellow squash circles, zucchini circles, unpeeled red potato chunks, cherry tomatoes, cucumber rounds

1 To make the Creamy Cheese Dip: In a medium-size bowl, using an electric mixer set on high speed, beat the cream cheese until smooth. Stir in the remaining dip ingredients except onion rings. Place in a small serving bowl, cover with plastic wrap and chill.

2 To prepare the Crudités: Half-fill a large saucepan with water and bring to a boil over high heat. Add the bell pepper, broccoli, carrots, celery, beans, mushrooms, peas, yellow squash and zucchini, one at a time, and blanch for 15 to 30 seconds or just until their color brightens. (*Do not overcook!*) Remove the vegetables with a slotted spoon, immediately plunge them into cold water, then drain well. Cook the potatoes in the same water for 15 minutes or until tender.

3 Arrange the blanched vegetables, potatoes, tomatoes and cucumbers in a circle on a large platter, leaving space in the center for the bowl of dip. Cover with plastic wrap and chill. To serve: Uncover, garnish with the onion rings and place the bowl of dip in the center.

Makes 2 cups dip

Nutritional Comparison Per Serving
(1 tablespoon)

Alpine Lace® Recipe		Traditional Recipe	
Calories	17	Calories	72
Calories from Fat	<1	Calories from Fat	67
Total Fat	0 g	Total Fat	8 g
Cholesterol	2 mg	Cholesterol	14 mg

Delicious discovery—a creamy dip that's free of fat and full of flavor!

REDUCED FAT

25% less fat than the traditional recipe

BRUSCHETTA AL POMODORO WITH TWO CHEESES

1 loaf (1 pound) country Italian bread, cut diagonally into 12 (1-inch) slices
2 teaspoons minced garlic
⅓ cup extra virgin olive oil
¼ teaspoon crushed red pepper flakes
4 large ripe plum tomatoes, thinly sliced crosswise
1 medium-size red onion, slivered
⅓ cup slivered fresh basil leaves or 1 tablespoon dried basil
Red wine vinegar
½ cup (2 ounces) shredded Alpine Lace® Fat Free Pasteurized Process Skim Milk Cheese Product— For Mozzarella Lovers
¼ cup (1 ounce) shredded Alpine Lace® Fat Free Pasteurized Process Skim Milk Cheese Product— For Parmesan Lovers

1 Preheat the broiler. Place the bread slices in a single layer on a baking sheet and toast both sides until golden brown. Immediately rub one side of each bread slice with the garlic.

2 In a small saucepan, heat the oil and red pepper flakes over medium heat until warm. Brush the top of each slice with the oil.

3 Top each bruschetta with 2 or 3 tomato slices, then add a few slivers of onion and basil. Sprinkle each with a little vinegar.

4 Sprinkle the bruschetta with the mozzarella and Parmesan. Broil 6 inches from the heat for 4 minutes or until cheese is bubbly.

Makes 12 servings

Nutritional Comparison Per Serving
(1 bruschetta)

Alpine Lace® Recipe		Traditional Recipe	
Calories	165	Calories	175
Calories from Fat	54	Calories from Fat	70
Total Fat	6 g	Total Fat	8 g
Cholesterol	4 mg	Cholesterol	5 mg

LOW FAT

BAKED MOZZARELLA STICKS

Butter-flavored nonstick
   cooking spray
12 ounces (2 blocks) Alpine
   Lace® Fat Free Pasteurized
   Process Skim Milk
   Cheese Product—
   For Mozzarella Lovers

½ cup egg substitute or 2 large
   eggs
1 cup Italian seasoned dry
   bread crumbs
¼ cup minced fresh parsley

1 Preheat the oven to 400°F. Spray 2 large baking sheets with the cooking spray.

2 Cut each block of cheese in half crosswise, then each half lengthwise into 3 equal sticks (about 3 × ¾ inches), making a total of 12 sticks.

3 In a medium-size bowl, whisk the egg substitute (or the whole eggs) until frothy. On a plate, toss the bread crumbs with the parsley.

4 Dip each cheese stick first into the egg substitute, then roll in the bread crumbs, pressing them slightly as you go. Arrange the cheese in a single layer on the baking sheets.

5 Spray the sticks lightly with the cooking spray. Bake for 10 minutes or until golden brown and crispy.   *Makes 12 cheese sticks*

Nutritional Comparison Per Serving
(1 mozzarella stick)

Alpine Lace® Recipe		Traditional Recipe	
Calories	87	Calories	221
Calories from Fat	8	Calories from Fat	163
Total Fat	1 g	Total Fat	18 g
Cholesterol	3 mg	Cholesterol	62 mg

SOUPS & SANDWICHES

Slim down your favorite soups by starting with stocks, vegetable purées and juices, then adding Alpine Lace® cheeses for extra flavor and creaminess. Trim down sandwiches by choosing Alpine Lace® cheeses and ham and stuffing them with plenty of veggies.

LOW FAT

MINESTRONE

1 tablespoon extra virgin olive oil
1 cup chopped red onion
2 teaspoons minced garlic
5 cups low sodium chicken broth
1 cup water
1 can (16 ounces) low sodium whole tomatoes, chopped and juices reserved
1 bay leaf
½ teaspoon salt or to taste
¼ teaspoon freshly ground black pepper

¾ cup uncooked ditalini pasta (mini macaroni)
2 packages (10 ounces each) frozen Italian vegetables
1 can (16 ounces) cannellini beans, rinsed and drained
⅓ cup slivered fresh basil leaves
1 cup (4 ounces) shredded Alpine Lace® Fat Free Pasteurized Process Skim Milk Cheese Product— For Parmesan Lovers

1 In an 8-quart Dutch oven, heat the oil over medium-high heat. Add the onion and garlic and sauté for 5 minutes or until the onion is soft.

2 Stir in the broth, water, tomatoes and their juices, the bay leaf, salt and pepper. Bring to a rolling boil, add the pasta and return to a rolling boil. Cook, uncovered, for 10 minutes or until the pasta is almost tender.

continued on page 20

A "big soup" that's a meal in itself— with 85% less fat than the traditional.

3 Stir in the vegetables and beans. Return to a boil. Reduce the heat to low and simmer 5 minutes longer or until the vegetables are tender. Remove the bay leaf and discard. Stir in the basil, sprinkle with the cheese and serve immediately.

Makes 10 first-course servings (1 cup each)
or 5 main-dish servings (2 cups each)

Nutritional Comparison Per Serving
(1 cup)

Alpine Lace® Recipe		Traditional Recipe	
Calories	167	Calories	324
Calories from Fat	18	Calories from Fat	130
Total Fat	2 g	Total Fat	14 g
Cholesterol	18 mg	Cholesterol	32 mg

LOW FAT

HAM AND CHEESE CALZONES

1 pound frozen bread dough, thawed
1 cup bottled marinara sauce
2 tablespoons low sodium tomato paste
1 tablespoon slivered fresh basil leaves or 1 teaspoon dried basil
1 cup (4 ounces) slivered Alpine Lace® Boneless Cooked Ham

1½ cups (6 ounces) shredded Alpine Lace® Fat Free Pasteurized Process Skim Milk Cheese Product— For Mozzarella Lovers
1 cup cooked small broccoli florets, drained
½ cup finely chopped red onion

1 Preheat the oven to 425°F. Spray 2 baking sheets with nonstick cooking spray. On a lightly floured surface, cut the dough into 6 equal pieces. Roll each piece into a 6-inch circle.

2 In a small bowl, blend the marinara sauce with the tomato paste and basil. Leaving a ½-inch border, spread the sauce over half of each dough circle. Then sprinkle with the ham, cheese and vegetables.

3 Moisten the edges of the dough with a little water, fold the dough over filling and seal with a fork. Place on the baking sheets. Bake at 450°F for 10 minutes. Serve hot!

Makes 6 calzones

Nutritional Comparison Per Serving
(1 calzone)

Alpine Lace® Recipe		Traditional Recipe	
Calories	312	Calories	356
Calories from Fat	43	Calories from Fat	108
Total Fat	5 g	Total Fat	12 g
Cholesterol	14 mg	Cholesterol	33 mg

LOW FAT

CHICKEN FAJITAS

2 tablespoons vegetable oil, divided
2 tablespoons fresh lime juice
2 teaspoons minced garlic
1 teaspoon dried oregano
½ teaspoon ground cumin
½ teaspoon red pepper flakes
¼ teaspoon salt
12 ounces boneless, skinless chicken breasts, pounded thin
4 flour tortillas (8-inch)
3 cups thin strips yellow onion, divided

12 tablespoons medium or hot salsa, divided
1 cup (4 ounces) shredded Alpine Lace® Fat Free Pasteurized Process Skim Milk Cheese Product— For Cheddar Lovers, divided
1 cup chopped ripe tomatoes
1 small avocado, peeled, seeded and chopped (optional)
2 tablespoons minced fresh cilantro

1 In a large shallow glass dish, mix 1 tablespoon of the oil with the lime juice, garlic, oregano, cumin, red pepper flakes and salt. Add the chicken and turn to coat. Cover, refrigerate and marinate for 30 minutes.

2 Preheat the grill (or broiler and broiler pan). Wrap the tortillas in foil and place on the grill away from the direct heat (or in the oven). Pour the marinade from the chicken into a small saucepan; bring to a boil.

3 Grill (or broil) the chicken, 4 inches from the heat, basting frequently with the hot marinade, for 6 to 8 minutes on each side or until the juices run clear when chicken is pierced with a fork. Transfer to a cutting board and slice into ¾-inch strips.

4 Meanwhile, in a medium-size nonstick skillet, sauté the onion in the remaining tablespoon of oil over medium-high heat for 8 minutes.

5 Unwrap the hot tortillas. For each fajita, spoon 2 tablespoons of salsa down the center of the tortilla. Top with a quarter of the chicken, onions and cheese. Roll up and place, seam side down, on a warm platter. Top each fajita with 1 tablespoon of the remaining salsa, some of the chopped tomatoes, avocado, if you wish, and the cilantro. *Makes 4 fajitas*

Nutritional Comparison Per Serving
(1 fajita)

Alpine Lace® Recipe		Traditional Recipe	
Calories	382	Calories	575
Calories from Fat	95	Calories from Fat	293
Total Fat	11 g	Total Fat	33 g
Cholesterol	54 mg	Cholesterol	102 mg

LOW FAT

PRIMAVERA PIZZA PIE

2 tablespoons yellow cornmeal
1 pound frozen bread dough, thawed
1½ cups (6 ounces) shredded Alpine Lace® Fat Free Pasteurized Process Skim Milk Cheese Product—For Mozzarella Lovers, divided
1 tablespoon extra virgin olive oil
1½ cups sliced mushrooms
1 teaspoon minced garlic
2 cups small broccoli florets or 1 large zucchini, trimmed and sliced
1 large red bell pepper, seeded and cut into thin strips

1 medium-size red onion, cut into strips
3 ripe plum tomatoes, thinly sliced
¼ cup (1 ounce) shredded Alpine Lace® Fat Free Pasteurized Process Skim Milk Cheese Product— For Parmesan Lovers
1 tablespoon snipped fresh oregano leaves or 1 teaspoon dried oregano
⅛ teaspoon crushed red pepper flakes

1 Preheat the oven to 425°F. Spray a 16-inch round pizza pan or a 15 × 10 × 2-inch baking pan with nonstick cooking spray and sprinkle with the cornmeal. Gently press the bread dough onto the bottom and up the sides of the pan. Sprinkle with 1 cup of the mozzarella.

2 Spray a nonstick skillet with the cooking spray, add the oil and heat over medium-high heat. Add the mushrooms and garlic and sauté for 5 minutes, then sprinkle over the top of the pizza.

3 In the same skillet, sauté the broccoli, bell pepper and onion for 5 minutes. Arrange vegetables on the pizza.

4 Top the pizza with the tomatoes and sprinkle with the remaining ½ cup of mozzarella, the Parmesan, oregano and red pepper flakes. Bake for 15 to 20 minutes or until the crust is golden brown.   *Makes 8 servings*

Nutritional Comparison Per Serving

Alpine Lace® Recipe		Traditional Recipe	
Calories	234	Calories	271
Calories from Fat	36	Calories from Fat	86
Total Fat	4 g	Total Fat	10 g
Cholesterol	4 mg	Cholesterol	19 mg

Serve this pizza proudly—
it has less than half the fat of a traditional slice!

LOW FAT

ONION SOUP WITH CROUTON CRUST

ONION SOUP

1 tablespoon vegetable oil

3 pounds large yellow onions, halved and thinly sliced (about 9 cups)

3 tablespoons all-purpose flour

⅔ cup apple brandy or water

5 cups low sodium beef stock or broth

2⅓ cups low sodium chicken stock or broth

1 tablespoon snipped fresh thyme leaves or 1 teaspoon dried thyme

1 teaspoon freshly ground black pepper

¼ teaspoon salt

CROUTON CRUST

8 slices (½ inch thick) whole wheat or white French bread

¾ cup (3 ounces) shredded Alpine Lace® Reduced Fat Swiss Cheese

1 To make the Onion Soup: Spray a 6-quart Dutch oven or stockpot with nonstick cooking spray. Add the oil and heat over medium-high heat.

2 Add the onions and cook, stirring occasionally, for about 10 minutes or until browned and caramelized. Stir in the flour, then the brandy. Bring to a boil.

3 Add both of the stocks, the thyme, pepper and salt. Return to a boil, then reduce the heat to low and simmer, uncovered, for 30 minutes.

4 While the soup simmers, make the Crouton Crust: Preheat the broiler. Place the bread slices on a baking sheet and broil until nicely browned on both sides. Remove the bread slices from the baking sheet and set aside.

5 Place 8 ovenproof soup bowls on the baking sheet. Ladle the soup into the bowls and top each with a crouton. Sprinkle crouton and soup with the cheese. Broil 6 inches from the heat for 1 to 2 minutes or until cheese is melted and bubbly.

Makes 8 first-course servings (1 cup each)

Nutritional Comparison Per Serving
(1 cup)

Alpine Lace® Recipe		Traditional Recipe	
Calories	273	Calories	305
Calories from Fat	50	Calories from Fat	62
Total Fat	5 g	Total Fat	7 g
Cholesterol	10 mg	Cholesterol	16 mg

A crock of onion soup with a crusty, low fat Swiss crouton on top.

LOW FAT

BARBECUED CHEESE BURGERS

BARBECUE SPREAD

¼ cup reduced calorie
    mayonnaise
¼ cup bottled barbecue sauce

¼ cup red or green pepper
    hamburger relish

BURGERS

1½ pounds ground lean turkey or
    ground beef round
⅓ cup bottled barbecue sauce
⅓ cup minced red onion
1 teaspoon hot red pepper
    sauce
½ teaspoon garlic salt

6 sesame seed hamburger buns,
    split
6 slices (1 ounce each)
    Alpine Lace® Fat Free
    Pasteurized Process Skim
    Milk Cheese Product—
    For Cheddar Lovers

1 To make the Barbecue Spread: In a small bowl, stir all of the spread ingredients together until well blended. Cover and refrigerate.

2 To make the Burgers: In a medium-size bowl, mix the turkey, barbecue sauce, onion, hot pepper sauce and garlic salt. Form into 6 patties (5 inches each), about 1¼ inches thick. Cover with plastic wrap and refrigerate for at least 30 minutes or overnight.

3 To cook the Burgers: Preheat the grill (or broiler). Grill over medium-hot coals (or broil) 4 inches from the heat for 4 minutes on each side for medium or until cooked the way you like them. Place the buns alongside the burgers for the last 5 minutes to heat, if you wish. Top each burger with a slice of cheese.

4 To serve, spread the insides of the buns with the Barbecue Spread and stuff each bun with a burger.

Makes 6 burgers

Nutritional Comparison Per Serving
(1 burger)

Alpine Lace® Recipe (with turkey)		Traditional Recipe (with beef)	
Calories	351	Calories	639
Calories from Fat	89	Calories from Fat	376
Total Fat	10 g	Total Fat	42 g
Cholesterol	63 mg	Cholesterol	134 mg

The All-American Burger—made from ground turkey and fat free Cheddar—weighs in at only one fourth the fat of the original.

Salad Tosses

Choose from salads filled with fresh-from-the-garden greens, unusual shapes of pasta, strips of meats or slices of veggies. Add an extra flavor dimension to salads by tossing in chunks or shreds of Alpine Lace® cheese—or swirl some cream cheese into the dressing.

FAT FREE

CREAMY GARLIC DRESSING

12 ounces (2 cartons) Alpine Lace® Fat Free Cream Cheese with Garlic & Herbs
½ cup 2% low fat milk
¼ cup fat free sour cream
2 tablespoons fresh lemon juice
1 tablespoon prepared horseradish
½ teaspoon freshly ground black pepper
Radish slices (optional)

1 In a food processor or blender, process all of the ingredients for 30 seconds or until well blended. Refrigerate until ready to serve. Garnish with the radish slices, if you wish.

2 Serve this dressing over vegetable or meat salads. It's also a great sauce for grilled meat, chicken and fish.

Makes 2 cups

Nutritional Comparison Per Serving
(2 tablespoons)

Alpine Lace® Recipe		Traditional Recipe	
Calories	34	Calories	88
Calories from Fat	2	Calories from Fat	72
Total Fat	0 g	Total Fat	8 g
Cholesterol	4 mg	Cholesterol	26 mg

Toss up a salad the no-fat way with a dressing made with Alpine Lace® fat free cream cheese, flavored with garlic and garden herbs aplenty.

REDUCED FAT

36% less fat than the traditional recipe

PASTA PESTO SALAD

PASTA SALAD

8 ounces three-color rotini
    pasta (corkscrews)
3 small bell peppers (1 green,
    1 red and 1 yellow), seeded
    and cut into thin strips
1 pint cherry tomatoes,
    stemmed and halved
    (2 cups)

6 ounces (1 block) Alpine
    Lace® Fat Free Pasteurized
    Process Skim Milk Cheese
    Product—For Mozzarella
    Lovers, cut into ½-inch
    cubes (1½ cups)
1 cup thin carrot circles
1 cup thin strips red onion
1 cup slivered fresh basil leaves

SPICY DRESSING

½ cup (2 ounces) shredded
    Alpine Lace® Fat Free
    Pasteurized Process Skim
    Milk Cheese Product—
    For Parmesan Lovers
⅓ cup firmly packed fresh
    parsley
⅓ cup extra virgin olive oil

⅓ cup red wine vinegar
2 large cloves garlic
1 tablespoon whole-grain Dijon
    mustard
¾ teaspoon freshly ground black
    pepper
½ teaspoon salt

1 To make the Pasta Salad: Cook the pasta according to package directions until al dente. Drain in a colander, rinse under cold water and drain again. Place the pasta in a large shallow pasta bowl and toss with the remaining salad ingredients.

2 To make the Spicy Dressing: In a food processor or blender, process all of the dressing ingredients for 30 seconds or until well blended.

3 Drizzle the dressing on the salad and toss to mix thoroughly. Cover with plastic wrap and refrigerate for 1 hour so that the flavors can blend, or let stand at room temperature for 1 hour.

Makes 12 side-dish servings or 6 main-dish servings

Nutritional Comparison Per Serving
(1 side-dish serving / 1 cup)

Alpine Lace® Recipe		Traditional Recipe	
Calories	173	Calories	208
Calories from Fat	59	Calories from Fat	99
Total Fat	7 g	Total Fat	11 g
Cholesterol	4 mg	Cholesterol	15 mg

A salad of pasta, pesto and fat free mozzarella. Buon appetito!

REDUCED FAT

43% less fat than the traditional recipe

CHICKEN CAESAR SALAD

WHOLE WHEAT CROUTONS

3 tablespoons extra virgin
    olive oil
3 tablespoons minced parsley
¾ teaspoon freshly ground black
    pepper
¼ teaspoon garlic salt or to taste
6 slices whole wheat bread,
    crusts trimmed

CAESAR DRESSING

1 large egg
⅓ cup fresh lemon juice
⅓ cup fresh orange juice
2 tablespoons extra virgin
    olive oil
1½ tablespoons Worcestershire
    sauce
3 large cloves garlic
¾ teaspoon dry mustard
¼ teaspoon salt or to taste
¼ teaspoon freshly ground black
    pepper
¼ cup (1 ounce) shredded
    Alpine Lace® Fat Free
    Pasteurized Process Skim
    Milk Cheese Product—
    For Parmesan Lovers

SALAD

2 pounds cooked boneless,
    skinless chicken breasts,
    cut into 1-inch-wide strips
8 cups washed and coarsely
    torn romaine lettuce
4 cups washed and coarsely
    torn Boston lettuce
4 cups washed and coarsely
    torn leaf lettuce
1 cup (4 ounces) shredded
    Alpine Lace® Fat Free
    Pasteurized Process Skim
    Milk Cheese Product—
    For Parmesan Lovers
6 anchovy fillets (optional)

1 To make the Whole Wheat Croutons: Preheat the oven to 350°F. In a cup, stir the oil, parsley, pepper and garlic salt together until well mixed. Brush on both sides of the bread slices, then cut each slice into 1-inch squares and arrange on a baking sheet. Bake, turning frequently, for 15 minutes or until nicely browned and crisp.

2 While the croutons are baking, make the Caesar Dressing: Half-fill a small saucepan with water and bring to a simmer over medium heat. Slide in the egg and cook for 5 minutes. Using a slotted spoon, plunge the egg into cold water, then peel when it is cool enough to handle. In a food processor or blender, process the egg with all of the remaining dressing ingredients for 30 seconds or until well blended.

3 To prepare the Salad: In a large salad bowl, toss the chicken with the lettuces and the croutons. Pour over the dressing and toss to coat thoroughly. Sprinkle with the Parmesan and garnish with the anchovies, if you wish. Serve immediately while the greens are still crisp.

Makes 12 side-dish servings or 6 main-dish servings

Nutritional Comparison Per Serving
(1 side-dish serving / 1½ cups)

Alpine Lace® Recipe		Traditional Recipe	
Calories	220	Calories	296
Calories from Fat	72	Calories from Fat	124
Total Fat	8 g	Total Fat	14 g
Cholesterol	81 mg	Cholesterol	102 mg

FAT FREE

THOUSAND ISLAND DRESSING

12 ounces (2 cartons) Alpine Lace® Fat Free Cream Cheese with Garden Vegetables
½ cup 2% low fat milk
⅓ cup fat free sour cream
¼ cup chili sauce

¼ cup minced dill pickles
2 to 3 tablespoons minced red onion
2 tablespoons fresh lemon juice
¼ teaspoon hot red pepper sauce

1 In a medium-size bowl, whisk all of the ingredients together until well blended. Refrigerate until ready to serve.

2 Serve this dressing over fish, meat or green salads. *Makes 2¼ cups*

Nutritional Comparison Per Serving
(2 tablespoons)

Alpine Lace® Recipe		Traditional Recipe	
Calories	30	Calories	84
Calories from Fat	2	Calories from Fat	68
Total Fat	0 g	Total Fat	8 g
Cholesterol	4 mg	Cholesterol	24 mg

REDUCED FAT

64% less fat than the traditional recipe

HEALTHY CHEF'S SALAD

PEPPER CRÈME DRESSING
⅔ cup reduced calorie
    mayonnaise
⅔ cup fat free sour cream
⅓ cup bottled chili sauce
⅓ cup chopped red bell pepper

¼ cup minced chives or green
    onions
2 tablespoons fresh lemon juice
½ teaspoon freshly ground black
    pepper

CHEF'S SALAD
12 cups washed and coarsely
    torn mixed salad greens
    (leaf lettuce, romaine and
    endive)
 1 small cucumber, halved
    lengthwise and thinly sliced
⅓ cup finely chopped green
    onions, divided
 1 cup cooked corn kernels
 1 cup cooked green peas
 3 cups peeled and grated
    carrots
 4 medium-size ripe tomatoes,
    cut into wedges

12 ounces skinless roasted
    turkey breast, cut into thin
    strips
 6 ounces Alpine Lace® Boneless
    Cooked Ham, cut into thin
    strips
 6 ounces Alpine Lace® Reduced
    Fat Swiss Cheese, cut into
    thin strips
 6 ounces roast beef, cut into
    thin strips (optional)
 2 large eggs, hard-cooked,
    peeled and thinly sliced
    (optional)

1 To make the Pepper Crème Dressing: In a medium-size bowl, whisk all of the dressing ingredients together until well blended.

2 To make the Chef's Salad: In a large, shallow salad bowl, toss the greens, cucumber, half of the green onions, the corn and peas. Mound the carrots in the center and arrange the tomatoes around the edge. In a spoke design, alternately arrange on the greens the turkey, ham and cheese, plus the beef and eggs, if you wish. Sprinkle with the remaining green onions and serve with the dressing.   *Makes 10 luncheon servings or 6 supper servings*

Nutritional Comparison Per Serving
(1 luncheon serving / 2 cups)

Alpine Lace® Recipe		Traditional Recipe	
Calories	262	Calories	429
Calories from Fat	95	Calories from Fat	249
Total Fat	10 g	Total Fat	28 g
Cholesterol	49 mg	Cholesterol	124 mg

A sensational chef's salad with less than half the fat of the traditional.

Pasta Perfect

Pasta dishes become perfect when made with Alpine Lace® cheeses. Toss fettuccine with a fat free cream cheese sauce, layer fat free mozzarella into a rice strata and blend fat free Parmesan into a sauce for manicotti. Buon appetito!

LOW FAT

ALPINE FETTUCCINE

½ pound white fettuccine,
  preferably fresh
½ pound green fettuccine,
  preferably fresh
1½ teaspoons extra virgin olive oil
1 cup sliced fresh mushrooms

1 cup chopped red bell pepper
½ cup skim milk
6 ounces (1 carton) Alpine Lace®
  Fat Free Cream Cheese
  with Garlic & Herbs

1 Cook the fettuccine according to package directions until al dente. Drain well and place in a large shallow pasta bowl. Toss with the oil and keep warm.

2 Meanwhile, spray a medium-size nonstick skillet with nonstick cooking spray. Add the mushrooms and bell pepper and sauté until soft. Toss with the fettuccine.

3 In a small saucepan, bring the milk to a boil over medium heat. Add the cream cheese and stir until melted. Toss with pasta and serve immediately.

*Makes 9 side-dish servings (1 cup each)
or 6 main-dish servings (1½ cups each)*

Nutritional Comparison Per Serving
(1 cup)

Alpine Lace® Recipe		Traditional Recipe	
Calories	228	Calories	315
Calories from Fat	26	Calories from Fat	130
Total Fat	3 g	Total Fat	15 g
Cholesterol	51 mg	Cholesterol	87 mg

A fabulous low fat version of Fettuccine Alfredo. Enjoy!

LOW FAT

STUFFED SHELLS

8 jumbo pasta shells (1 pound)
6 ounces (1 carton) Alpine
    Lace® Fat Free Cream
    Cheese with Garlic & Herbs
¼ cup fat free sour cream
½ cup Italian seasoned dry
    bread crumbs

2 tablespoons slivered fresh
    basil leaves
1 small ripe tomato, finely
    chopped
1 cup marinara sauce (bottled
    or refrigerated), heated
    (optional)

1 Cook the pasta shells according to package directions until al dente. Drain well, arrange on a serving platter and keep warm.

2 Meanwhile, in a small saucepan, stir the cream cheese and the sour cream over low heat until hot. *(Do not boil!)* Remove from the heat and stir in the bread crumbs and basil.

3 Using a small spoon, stuff each shell with the cheese mixture, then top with a few pieces of tomato. Serve immediately with the marinara sauce, if you wish.

Makes 4 servings (2 stuffed shells each)

Nutritional Comparison Per Serving
(2 stuffed shells)

Alpine Lace® Recipe		Traditional Recipe	
Calories	543	Calories	655
Calories from Fat	23	Calories from Fat	184
Total Fat	3 g	Total Fat	21 g
Cholesterol	8 mg	Cholesterol	53 mg

LOW FAT

MAC & CHEESE WITH CRUNCHY HERB CRUST

1 pound elbow macaroni
1 cup chopped yellow onion
1 cup chopped red bell pepper
1 cup herb seasoned dry
    stuffing, crumbled, divided
1½ cups skim milk
12 ounces (2 cartons) Alpine
    Lace® Fat Free Cream
    Cheese with Garlic & Herbs

1 teaspoon low sodium
    Worcestershire sauce
¼ teaspoon ground nutmeg
    Paprika
2 tablespoons extra virgin
    olive oil

1 Preheat the oven to 350°F. Spray a 12-inch round or oval ovenproof baking dish with nonstick cooking spray. Cook the macaroni according to package directions until al dente. Drain well, place in the baking dish and keep warm.

2 Spray a large nonstick skillet with the nonstick cooking spray and heat over medium-high heat for 1 minute. Add the onion and bell pepper and sauté for 5 minutes or until soft. Toss with the macaroni and ½ cup of the stuffing.

3 In a small saucepan, bring the milk to a boil over medium heat. Add the cream cheese and stir until melted. Remove from the heat and stir in the Worcestershire and nutmeg. Pour over the macaroni mixture. *(Do not stir.)*

4 Top with the remaining ½ cup of stuffing, then sprinkle with the paprika and olive oil. Cover tightly with foil and bake for 30 minutes or until bubbly and hot. Serve hot!

Makes 8 servings

Nutritional Comparison Per Serving

Alpine Lace® Recipe		Traditional Recipe	
Calories	195	Calories	312
Calories from Fat	36	Calories from Fat	180
Total Fat	4 g	Total Fat	21 g
Cholesterol	8 mg	Cholesterol	53 mg

LOW FAT

SHRIMP PRIMAVERA

8 ounces capelli d'angelo (angel hair pasta), preferably fresh
1½ pounds medium-size fresh shrimp, shelled and deveined, with tails removed
4 teaspoons minced garlic
2 cups thin carrot sticks (about 3 inches long)
2 cups thin strips red bell peppers (about 3 inches long)
2 cups thinly sliced ripe plum tomatoes

2 cups thin strips zucchini (about 3 inches long)
½ teaspoon crushed red pepper flakes
½ cup skim milk
12 ounces (2 cartons) Alpine Lace® Fat Free Cream Cheese with Garlic & Herbs
1 cup slivered fresh basil leaves or 1 cup minced fresh parsley plus 2 tablespoons dried basil
Sprigs of fresh basil (optional)

1 Cook the pasta according to package directions until al dente. Drain, place in a large shallow pasta bowl and keep warm.

2 Half-fill the same saucepan with water, bring to a boil and cook the shrimp just until pink. Toss with the pasta and keep warm.

3 Spray a large nonstick skillet with nonstick cooking spray and heat over medium-high heat for 1 minute. Add the garlic and sauté for 1 minute. Stir in the carrots, bell peppers, tomatoes, zucchini and red pepper flakes. Cook, stirring constantly, for 5 minutes or until carrots are crisp-tender. Toss with the pasta and shrimp.

4 In a small saucepan, bring the milk to a boil over medium heat. Add the cream cheese and stir until melted. Toss with the pasta mixture, then sprinkle with the basil. Garnish with basil sprigs, if you wish. Serve hot!

Makes 6 servings

Nutritional Comparison Per Serving

Alpine Lace® Recipe		Traditional Recipe	
Calories	288	Calories	433
Calories from Fat	25	Calories from Fat	211
Total Fat	3 g	Total Fat	24 g
Cholesterol	198 mg	Cholesterol	253 mg

Fresh shrimp and veggies are tossed with angel hair pasta and a fat free cream cheese sauce.

LOW FAT

CHEESE & RICE STRATA

2 tablespoons extra virgin
    olive oil
1 cup finely chopped celery
1 cup finely chopped onion
1 teaspoon snipped fresh
    oregano leaves or
    ½ teaspoon dried oregano
1 cup white basmati rice
3 cups low sodium chicken
    broth, divided
2 cups (8 ounces) shredded
    Alpine Lace® Fat Free
    Pasteurized Process Skim
    Milk Cheese Product—
    For Mozzarella Lovers

1 cup chopped Alpine Lace®
    Boneless Cooked Ham
¼ cup (1 ounce) shredded
    Alpine Lace® Fat Free
    Pasteurized Process Skim
    Milk Cheese Product—
    For Parmesan Lovers
¼ cup firmly packed fresh basil
    leaves

1 Preheat the oven to 350°F. Spray a 2-quart baking dish with nonstick cooking spray.

2 In a large saucepan, heat the oil over medium-high heat and sauté the celery and onion for 5 minutes or until soft. Stir in the oregano, rice and 2 cups of the broth. Bring to a gentle boil, reduce heat and simmer, uncovered, stirring constantly, for 10 to 15 minutes or until most of the broth has been absorbed.

3 Gradually add the remaining cup of broth, stirring occasionally. Continue to cook until the rice is almost tender.

4 In a small bowl, toss together the mozzarella and ham. Spread a third of the rice mixture over the bottom of the baking dish, sprinkle with half of the mozzarella mixture. Repeat layers. Top with the remaining third of the rice mixture. Bake for 20 minutes or until hot and the cheese is melted.

5 In a food processor or blender, process the Parmesan and basil for 30 seconds or until finely chopped. Sprinkle over the strata and serve immediately.

Makes 8 servings

Nutritional Comparison Per Serving

Alpine Lace® Recipe		Traditional Recipe	
Calories	203	Calories	265
Calories from Fat	38	Calories from Fat	113
Total Fat	4 g	Total Fat	13 g
Cholesterol	14 mg	Cholesterol	35 mg

LOW FAT

STUFFED MANICOTTI

MANICOTTI

12 ounces manicotti (about 12)

2 cups (8 ounces) shredded Alpine Lace® Reduced Sodium Low Moisture Part-Skim Mozzarella Cheese

2 cups part-skim ricotta cheese

⅓ cup slivered fresh basil leaves or 2 tablespoons dried basil

¼ cup Italian seasoned dry bread crumbs

PARMESAN SAUCE

1½ cups 2% low fat milk

2 tablespoons all-purpose flour

1 teaspoon Worcestershire sauce

¼ teaspoon crushed red pepper flakes

1 cup (4 ounces) shredded Alpine Lace® Fat Free Pasteurized Process Skim Milk Cheese Product—For Parmesan Lovers, divided

1 Preheat the oven to 375°F. Spray a 13 × 9 × 2-inch baking dish with nonstick cooking spray. Prepare the manicotti according to package directions, transfer to paper towels and keep warm.

2 To stuff the Manicotti: In a small bowl, stir together the mozzarella cheese, ricotta cheese, basil and bread crumbs. Using a small spoon, stuff the manicotti with the cheese mixture. Arrange in a single layer in the baking dish.

3 To make the Parmesan Sauce: In a medium-size saucepan, combine the milk, flour, Worcestershire and red pepper flakes. Bring to a boil, stirring constantly, over medium-high heat until the sauce thickens. Stir in ½ cup of the Parmesan.

4 Pour the sauce over the manicottti, completely covering the top. Sprinkle with the remaining ½ cup of the Parmesan. Cover with foil and bake for 20 minutes or until bubbly.

5 Uncover, turn the oven to broil and broil 4 inches from the heat for 2 minutes or until golden brown.

Makes 12 first-course servings (1 manicotti)
or 6 main-dish servings (2 manicotti)

Nutritional Comparison Per Serving
(1 manicotti)

Alpine Lace® Recipe		Traditional Recipe	
Calories	257	Calories	300
Calories from Fat	70	Calories from Fat	121
Total Fat	8 g	Total Fat	14 g
Cholesterol	37 mg	Cholesterol	46 mg

WHAT'S FOR DINNER?

In the mood for a juicy roast, a slice of meat loaf or a fish fillet? You'll find them here, all with less fat than traditional versions. Each is made extra special with an Alpine Lace® cheese—from grates of fat free Parmesan to slices of reduced fat Swiss to shreds of reduced fat Cheddar.

LOW FAT

BUTTERFLIED SHRIMP PARMESAN

1½ pounds large shrimp
1 cup (4 ounces) shredded Alpine Lace® Fat Free Pasteurized Process Skim Milk Cheese Product— For Parmesan Lovers
¼ cup Italian seasoned dry bread crumbs
2 tablespoons unsalted butter substitute

¾ cup chopped red bell pepper
½ cup thinly sliced green onions
1 tablespoon minced garlic
⅛ teaspoon crushed red pepper flakes or to taste
⅓ cup minced fresh parsley
6 tablespoons 2% low fat milk

1 Peel the shrimp, leaving the tails on. Then butterfly each shrimp by cutting it along the outer curved edge almost all the way through. Open the shrimp up like a book and remove the dark vein. In a small bowl, toss the cheese with the bread crumbs and set aside.

2 In a large nonstick skillet, melt the butter over medium-high heat. Add the bell pepper, green onions, garlic and red pepper flakes and cook for 5 minutes or until soft. Add the shrimp and sauté for 5 minutes or just until the shrimp turn pink and opaque. Stir in the parsley.

continued on page 46

Shrimp in a hurry—made the healthy way with fat free Parmesan!

3 In a small saucepan, bring the milk just to a boil, then stir into the shrimp mixture. Stir in the cheese mixture and cook until the cheese is melted. Serve immediately. *Makes 4 servings*

Nutritional Comparison Per Serving

Alpine Lace® Recipe		Traditional Recipe	
Calories	312	Calories	423
Calories from Fat	79	Calories from Fat	168
Total Fat	9 g	Total Fat	19 g
Cholesterol	281 mg	Cholesterol	304 mg

REDUCED FAT

56% less fat than the traditional recipe

STUFFED SIRLOIN ROAST

1 boneless sirloin steak, 2 inches thick (about 3 pounds), well trimmed
½ teaspoon salt
½ teaspoon freshly ground black pepper
2 tablespoons unsalted butter substitute
8 ounces mushrooms, chopped
2 teaspoons minced garlic

1 cup (4 ounces) shredded Alpine Lace® Reduced Fat Swiss Cheese
1 tablespoon snipped fresh rosemary leaves or 1 teaspoon dried rosemary
2 teaspoons snipped fresh thyme leaves or ½ teaspoon dried thyme
Sprigs of fresh rosemary

1 Preheat the oven to 350°F. Fit a large roasting pan with a rack. Cut the steak horizontally, with a sharp pointed knife, almost, but not completely, through. Open the steak like a book. Sprinkle with the salt and pepper.

2 In a medium-size skillet, melt the butter over medium-high heat. Add the mushrooms and garlic and sauté for 5 minutes or until all the liquid has evaporated. Spread the mushroom mixture evenly on the steak. In a small bowl, toss the cheese with the rosemary and thyme and sprinkle on top of the mushroom mixture.

3 Starting with one of the wide ends, roll up the steak, jelly-roll style. Tie with a piece of cotton string at 2-inch intervals. Place the roast, seam side down, on the rack. Bake, uncovered, for 45 minutes for rare (55 minutes for medium-rare) or until it's the way you like it. Decorate with the rosemary sprigs and serve immediately! *Makes 12 servings*

Nutritional Comparison Per Serving
(¾-inch slice)

Alpine Lace® Recipe		Traditional Recipe	
Calories	202	Calories	376
Calories from Fat	102	Calories from Fat	225
Total Fat	11 g	Total Fat	25 g
Cholesterol	63 mg	Cholesterol	116 mg

REDUCED FAT

52% less fat than the traditional recipe

HAM ROLLS WITH FRESH ASPARAGUS

1 pound trimmed fresh
asparagus spears or frozen
asparagus spears, thawed
and drained
8 slices (1 ounce each)
Alpine Lace® Boneless
Cooked Ham
½ cup thin strips red bell pepper
2 cups (8 ounces) shredded
Alpine Lace® Reduced Fat
Swiss Cheese, divided

1½ cups 2% low fat milk
2 tablespoons all-purpose flour
2 teaspoons snipped fresh dill
or ½ teaspoon dill weed
¼ teaspoon white pepper
Paprika

1 Preheat the oven to 375°F. Spray an 8-inch square baking dish with nonstick cooking spray.

2 To assemble the ham rolls: In a large saucepan, bring 1 inch of water to a boil. Add the asparagus and steam just until crisp-tender; drain well. Lay out the slices of ham. Place 1 or 2 asparagus spears and a few strips of bell pepper in the center of each and sprinkle with 1 tablespoon of the cheese, reserving 1½ cups of cheese. Roll up and place, seam side down, in the dish.

3 To make the Swiss-dill sauce: In a medium-size saucepan, combine the milk, flour, dill and white pepper. Stir over medium-high heat until mixture boils. Reduce the heat and stir until thickened. Stir in the reserved 1½ cups cheese until melted. Pour over the ham rolls and sprinkle with the paprika.

4 Cover with foil and bake for 15 minutes. Remove the foil and bake 15 minutes more or until the sauce is bubbly. Turn the oven to broil and broil 4 inches from the heat for 3 minutes or just until golden brown. Serve hot.

Makes 8 servings

Nutritional Comparison Per Serving
(1 ham roll)

Alpine Lace® Recipe		Traditional Recipe	
Calories	167	Calories	279
Calories from Fat	90	Calories from Fat	186
Total Fat	10 g	Total Fat	21 g
Cholesterol	41 mg	Cholesterol	69 mg

LOW FAT

CHICKEN ENCHILADAS

1¾ cups fat free sour cream
½ cup chopped green onions
⅓ cup minced fresh cilantro
1 tablespoon minced fresh
  jalapeño chili pepper
1 teaspoon ground cumin
1 tablespoon vegetable oil
12 ounces boneless, skinless
  chicken breasts, cut into
  3 × 1-inch strips

1 teaspoon minced garlic
8 flour tortillas (8-inch)
1 cup (4 ounces) shredded
  Alpine Lace® Reduced Fat
  Cheddar Cheese
1 cup bottled chunky salsa
  (medium or hot)
1 small ripe tomato, chopped
  Sprigs of cilantro (optional)

1 Preheat the oven to 350°F. Spray a 13 × 9 × 3-inch baking dish with nonstick cooking spray.

2 In a small bowl, mix together the sour cream, green onions, cilantro, jalapeño pepper and cumin.

3 Spray a large nonstick skillet with the cooking spray, pour in the oil and heat over medium-high heat. Add the chicken and garlic and sauté for 4 minutes or until the juices run clear when the chicken is pierced with a fork.

4 Divide the chicken strips among the 8 tortillas, placing them down the center of the tortillas. Top with the sour cream mixture, then roll them up and place them, seam side down, in the baking dish.

5 Sprinkle with the cheese, cover with foil and bake for 30 minutes or until bubbly. Spoon the salsa in a strip down the center and sprinkle the salsa with the tomato. Garnish with the sprigs of cilantro, if you wish. Serve hot!

Makes 8 servings

Nutritional Comparison Per Serving
(1 enchilada)

Alpine Lace® Recipe		Traditional Recipe	
Calories	247	Calories	381
Calories from Fat	59	Calories from Fat	200
Total Fat	6 g	Total Fat	23 g
Cholesterol	33 mg	Cholesterol	73 mg

Enchiladas rolled up with chicken, reduced fat Cheddar and all of the traditional tastes, but with only one fourth the fat!

LOW FAT

STUFFED CHICKEN BREASTS À LA FRANÇAISE

6 boneless, skinless chicken breast halves, with pockets (6 ounces each)

6 ounces (1 carton) Alpine Lace® Fat Free Cream Cheese with Garlic & Herbs

½ cup finely chopped green onions (tops only)

2 teaspoons snipped fresh rosemary leaves or ¾ teaspoon dried rosemary

½ cup all-purpose flour

1 teaspoon freshly ground black pepper

⅓ cup low sodium chicken broth

⅓ cup dry white wine or low sodium chicken broth

8 sprigs fresh rosemary, about 3 inches long (optional)

1 Preheat the oven to 350°F. Spray a 13 × 9 × 2-inch baking dish with nonstick cooking spray. Rinse the chicken and pat dry with paper towels. In a medium-size bowl, mix the cream cheese with the green onions and rosemary until well blended. Stuff the pockets of the chicken breasts with this mixture.

2 On a piece of wax paper, blend the flour and pepper. Roll each chicken breast in the seasoned flour, then arrange in the baking dish. Pour over the broth and the wine.

3 Cover the dish tightly with foil and bake for 30 minutes. Uncover and bake 10 minutes more or until the juices run clear when the thickest piece of chicken is pierced with a fork.

4 Transfer the chicken to a serving platter and garnish each with a sprig of rosemary, if you wish.

Makes 6 servings

Nutritional Comparison Per Serving
(½ chicken breast)

Alpine Lace® Recipe		Traditional Recipe	
Calories	274	Calories	530
Calories from Fat	23	Calories from Fat	257
Total Fat	3 g	Total Fat	29 g
Cholesterol	107 mg	Cholesterol	174 mg

Stuff chicken breasts the low fat way with fat free cream cheese!

REDUCED FAT

64% less fat than the traditional recipe

STUFFED PORK TENDERLOIN

2 teaspoons minced garlic
2 teaspoons snipped fresh
    rosemary leaves or
    ½ teaspoon dried rosemary
2 teaspoons snipped fresh
    thyme leaves or ½ teaspoon
    dried thyme
1 teaspoon salt
½ teaspoon freshly ground black
    pepper
1 boneless end-cut rolled pork
    loin with tenderloin
    attached (4 pounds), tied

1 tablespoon unsalted butter
    substitute
1 cup thin strips yellow onion
2 large tart apples, peeled,
    cored and thinly sliced
    (2 cups)
10 thin slices (½ ounce each)
    Alpine Lace® Reduced Fat
    Swiss Cheese
1 cup apple cider or apple juice

1 Preheat the oven to 325°F. Fit a 13 × 9 × 3-inch baking pan with a rack. In a small bowl, combine the garlic, rosemary, thyme, salt and pepper. Untie and unroll the pork loin, laying it flat. Rub half of the spice mixture onto the pork.

2 In a medium-size skillet, melt the butter over medium-high heat. Add the onion and apples and sauté for 5 minutes or until soft. Spread this mixture evenly on the pork and cover with the cheese slices.

3 Starting from one of the widest ends, re-roll the pork, jelly-roll style. Tie the roast with cotton string at 1-inch intervals and rub the outside with the remaining spice mixture. Place the roast on the rack in the pan and pour the apple cider over it.

4 Roast, uncovered, basting frequently with the pan drippings, for 2 to 2½ hours or until an instant-read thermometer inserted in the thickest part registers 160°F. Let the roast stand for 15 minutes before slicing.

Makes 16 servings

Nutritional Comparison Per Serving
(½-inch slice)

Alpine Lace® Recipe		Traditional Recipe	
Calories	190	Calories	406
Calories from Fat	89	Calories from Fat	251
Total Fat	10 g	Total Fat	28 g
Cholesterol	57 mg	Cholesterol	113 mg

*A Swiss surprise—fresh herbs, onions, apples and reduced fat
Swiss cheese swirled inside fresh-roasted pork.*

LOW FAT

SOLE FLORENTINE

1¼ pounds washed fresh spinach or 2 packages (10 ounces each) frozen spinach, thawed
¼ teaspoon salt or to taste
¼ teaspoon white pepper or to taste
½ cup dry white wine or low sodium chicken broth
1½ pounds boneless sole fillets (about 6)
6 ounces (1 carton) Alpine Lace® Fat Free Cream Cheese with Garlic & Herbs

½ cup fat free sour cream
3 tablespoons unsalted butter substitute
¼ cup (1 ounce) shredded Alpine Lace® Fat Free Pasteurized Process Skim Milk Cheese Product—For Parmesan Lovers
Paprika

1 Preheat the oven to 350°F. Spray an 8-inch square baking dish with nonstick cooking spray.

2 In a large saucepan, bring 1 inch of water to a boil. Add the spinach and steam just until wilted; drain well. Line the bottom of the baking dish with the cooked spinach, then sprinkle with the salt and pepper.

3 In a large nonstick skillet, bring the wine to a simmer over medium-high heat. Slide in the sole fillets, cover and poach for 4 minutes or until opaque and springy to the touch. Using a slotted spatula, carefully remove the fillets and arrange on top of the spinach.

4 In a small bowl, blend the cream cheese with the sour cream, then spread on top of the fillets.

5 Dot with the butter and sprinkle with the Parmesan and paprika. Bake, uncovered, for 20 minutes or until the cheese mixture is bubbly. Serve immediately.

Makes 6 servings

Nutritional Comparison Per Serving
(1 fillet of sole)

Alpine Lace® Recipe		Traditional Recipe	
Calories	232	Calories	356
Calories from Fat	70	Calories from Fat	225
Total Fat	9 g	Total Fat	25 g
Cholesterol	8 mg	Cholesterol	60 mg

REDUCED FAT

50% less fat than the traditional recipe

MEAT LOAF WITH PARMESAN CRUST

1 tablespoon vegetable oil

1 cup chopped yellow onion

1 cup chopped green bell pepper

2 teaspoons minced garlic

2 pounds ground lean turkey or ground beef round

¼ cup egg substitute or 1 large egg, beaten

⅓ cup bottled chili sauce

2 cups seasoned bread crumbs, divided

½ teaspoon freshly ground black pepper

¾ cup (3 ounces) shredded Alpine Lace® Fat Free Pasteurized Process Skim Milk Cheese Product— For Parmesan Lovers

½ cup firmly packed parsley leaves

3 strips turkey bacon (optional)

1 Preheat the oven to 350°F. Spray a 9 × 5 × 3-inch loaf pan with nonstick cooking spray. In a large skillet, heat the oil over medium-high heat. Add the onion, bell pepper and garlic and sauté for 5 minutes or until tender. Transfer to a large bowl.

2 Add the turkey, egg substitute (or the egg), chili sauce, 1½ cups of the bread crumbs and the black pepper to the onion mixture. Mix with your hands until well blended.

3 In a food processor or blender, process the Parmesan, parsley and the remaining ½ cup of bread crumbs for 30 seconds or until fine crumbs form. Mix into the turkey mixture.

4 Transfer the turkey mixture to the pan and pat into a loaf, mounding it slightly in the center. Place the bacon strips diagonally across the top of the loaf, if you wish.

5 Bake for 1 hour or until an instant-read thermometer inserted into the center registers 165°F. Loosely cover meat loaf with foil during the last 15 minutes. Transfer to a warm platter, let stand for 10 minutes, then slice and serve.

Makes 12 servings

Nutritional Comparison Per Serving
(¾-inch slice)

Alpine Lace® Recipe (with turkey)		Traditional Recipe (with beef)	
Calories	212	Calories	291
Calories from Fat	71	Calories from Fat	144
Total Fat	8 g	Total Fat	16 g
Cholesterol	61 mg	Cholesterol	71 mg

LOW FAT

MARYLAND CRAB CAKES

1¼ pounds lump crab meat, picked over and flaked

¾ cup plain dry bread crumbs, divided

1 cup (4 ounces) shredded Alpine Lace® Reduced Fat Swiss Cheese

¼ cup plain low fat yogurt

⅓ cup finely chopped green onions

¼ cup minced fresh parsley

2 tablespoons fresh lemon juice

1 teaspoon minced garlic

½ teaspoon hot red pepper sauce

¼ cup egg substitute or 1 large egg, beaten

Butter-flavor nonstick cooking spray

2 large lemons, thinly sliced

1 In a large bowl, lightly toss the crab with ¼ cup of the bread crumbs, the cheese, yogurt, green onions, parsley, lemon juice, garlic and hot pepper sauce. Gently stir in the egg substitute (or the whole egg).

2 Form the mixture into twelve 3-inch patties, using about ⅓ cup of crab mixture for each. Spray both sides of the patties with the cooking spray.

3 On wax paper, spread out the remaining ½ cup of bread crumbs. Coat each patty with the crumbs, pressing lightly, then refrigerate for 1 hour.

4 Preheat the oven to 400°F. Spray a baking sheet with the cooking spray. Place the crab cakes on the baking sheet and bake for 20 minutes or until golden brown and crispy, turning once halfway through. Serve immediately with the lemon slices.

Makes 6 servings (2 crab cakes each)

Nutritional Comparison Per Serving
(2 crab cakes)

Alpine Lace® Recipe		Traditional Recipe	
Calories	215	Calories	266
Calories from Fat	53	Calories from Fat	104
Total Fat	6 g	Total Fat	12 g
Cholesterol	54 mg	Cholesterol	105 mg

*Crab cakes straight from Maryland's Eastern Shore—
with half the fat of the traditional ones, thanks to oven frying.*

EAT YOUR VEGETABLES!

Here's a natural way to get your vegetables—and enjoy them, too! Add the great taste of Alpine Lace® cheeses and still keep the fat and calories in control. Try such tempting dishes as Iowa Corn Pudding, Double Baked Potatoes and Eggplant Parmigiana the low fat way.

LOW FAT

IOWA CORN PUDDING

½ cup egg substitute or
    2 large eggs
2 large egg whites
3 tablespoons all-purpose flour
1 tablespoon sugar
½ teaspoon freshly ground black
    pepper
1 can (16½ ounces) cream-style
    corn
2 cups fresh corn kernels or
    frozen corn, thawed and
    drained

1 cup (4 ounces) shredded
    Alpine Lace® American
    Flavor Pasteurized Process
    Cheese Product
½ cup finely chopped red bell
    pepper
⅓ cup 2% low fat milk
1 tablespoon unsalted butter
    substitute
¼ teaspoon paprika
    Sprigs of fresh parsley

1 Preheat the oven to 350°F. Spray an 8-inch round baking dish with nonstick cooking spray. (A deep-dish pie plate works well.) Place in the oven to heat.

2 Meanwhile, in a large bowl, using an electric mixer set on high, beat the egg substitute (or the whole eggs) and egg whites with the flour, sugar and black pepper until smooth. Stir in the creamed corn, corn kernels, cheese, bell pepper and milk. Pour into the hot baking dish.

continued on page 60

A creamy corn pudding with one third less fat than traditional versions.

3 Dot with the butter and sprinkle with the paprika. Bake, uncovered, for 55 minutes or until set. Let stand for 15 minutes before serving. Garnish with the parsley.

Makes 6 servings

Nutritional Comparison Per Serving

Alpine Lace® Recipe		Traditional Recipe	
Calories	226	Calories	255
Calories from Fat	59	Calories from Fat	95
Total Fat	6 g	Total Fat	11 g
Cholesterol	17 mg	Cholesterol	96 mg

FAT FREE

DOUBLE BAKED POTATOES

4 medium-size Idaho baking
   potatoes (2 pounds)
½ cup skim milk
12 ounces (2 cartons) Alpine
   Lace® Fat Free Cream
   Cheese with Garden
   Vegetables

¾ teaspoon freshly ground black
   pepper
2 large egg whites
1 tablespoon snipped fresh
   rosemary leaves or
   1 teaspoon dried rosemary
¼ teaspoon paprika

1 Preheat the oven to 400°F. Scrub the potatoes and pierce the skins with a sharp knife. Place the potatoes on the middle oven rack and bake for 1 hour or until soft.

2 Reduce the oven temperature to 375°F. Cut a thin slice off the top of each potato. Using a small spoon, carefully scoop the pulp into a large bowl, leaving an ⅛-inch-thick shell. In a small saucepan, bring the milk to a boil over medium heat. Add the cream cheese and pepper and stir until melted.

3 Using an electric mixer set on low, break up the potato pulp. Add the hot cheese mixture, and beat on high until blended. Add the egg whites and beat until fluffy and almost smooth. (A few lumps are fine!)

4 Spoon the potato mixture into the shells and place on a baking sheet. Sprinkle with the rosemary and paprika. Bake for 20 minutes or until hot and puffy. Serve immediately.

Makes 4 servings

Nutritional Comparison Per Serving
(1 potato)

Alpine Lace® Recipe		Traditional Recipe	
Calories	256	Calories	474
Calories from Fat	3	Calories from Fat	279
Total Fat	0 g	Total Fat	31 g
Cholesterol	16 mg	Cholesterol	98 mg

LOW FAT

EGGPLANT PARMIGIANA

2 cups plain dry bread crumbs
1 cup (4 ounces) shredded
    Alpine Lace® Fat Free
    Pasteurized Process Skim
    Milk Cheese Product—
    For Parmesan Lovers
2 tablespoons Italian seasoning
2 teaspoons minced garlic,
    divided
2 medium-size unpeeled
    eggplants (2 pounds), cut
    crosswise into ½-inch-thick
    slices
2 egg whites, lightly beaten
2 tablespoons olive oil, divided

1½ cups thin strips red onion
1 can (28 ounces) crushed
    tomatoes in purée,
    undrained
⅓ cup water
½ cup slivered fresh basil leaves
1 teaspoon sugar
¼ teaspoon red pepper flakes
¼ teaspoon salt
2 cups (8 ounces) shredded
    Alpine Lace® Fat Free
    Pasteurized Process Skim
    Milk Cheese Product—
    For Mozzarella Lovers
¼ cup minced fresh parsley

1 Preheat the oven to 375°F. Spray 2 baking sheets and a 13 × 9 × 3-inch baking dish with nonstick cooking spray. In a food processor or blender, process the bread crumbs, Parmesan, Italian seasoning and 1 teaspoon of the garlic for 30 seconds. Spread on a plate.

2 Dip the eggplant slices into the egg whites, coat both sides with the crumb mixture, then arrange in a single layer on the baking sheets. Drizzle with 1 tablespoon of the oil. Bake the eggplant for 40 minutes or until crisp, turning the slices over once. Remove the eggplant from the oven and reduce the temperature to 350°F.

3 While the eggplant bakes, make the sauce: In a large skillet, heat the remaining tablespoon of the oil over medium-high heat. Add the onion and the remaining teaspoon of garlic and sauté for 5 minutes or until soft. Stir in the tomatoes and their purée, the water, basil, sugar, red pepper flakes and salt. Simmer, uncovered, for 5 minutes.

4 In the baking dish, layer a third of the eggplant slices, a third of the sauce and a third of the mozzarella cheese; repeat 2 times. Bake for 30 minutes or until bubbly; sprinkle with the parsley.   *Makes 8 servings*

Nutritional Comparison Per Serving

Alpine Lace® Recipe		Traditional Recipe	
Calories	264	Calories	342
Calories from Fat	46	Calories from Fat	134
Total Fat	5 g	Total Fat	15 g
Cholesterol	12 mg	Cholesterol	32 mg

REDUCED FAT

REDUCED FAT

47% less fat than the traditional recipe

GREEN 'N' WHITE VEGETABLES AU GRATIN

VEGETABLES

¼ teaspoon salt
2 pounds fresh broccoli, separated into florets and trimmed

1 medium-size head cauliflower, separated into florets and trimmed (about 2 pounds)

AU GRATIN SAUCE

1½ cups 2% low fat milk
2 tablespoons all-purpose flour
1 teaspoon Worcestershire sauce
¼ teaspoon crushed red pepper flakes

⅛ teaspoon ground nutmeg
2 cups (8 ounces) shredded Alpine Lace® Reduced Fat Cheddar Cheese

1 To prepare the Vegetables: Half-fill a large saucepan with water, add the salt and bring to a boil over high heat.

2 Add the broccoli and cook, uncovered, for 10 minutes or until tender. Using a slotted spoon, transfer the broccoli to a colander to drain. Arrange the broccoli around the edge of a large round platter and keep warm.

3 To the same boiling water, add the cauliflower florets and cook, uncovered, for 8 minutes or until tender. Drain and arrange the cauliflower in the center of the platter.

4 While the vegetables cook, make the Au Gratin Sauce: In a medium-size saucepan, combine the milk, flour, Worcestershire, red pepper flakes and nutmeg. Bring to a boil, stirring constantly, over medium-high heat.

5 Reduce the heat to medium and stir until thickened. Then add the cheese and stir until melted. Drizzle the sauce over the vegetables and serve immediately.

Makes 6 servings

Nutritional Comparison Per Serving

Alpine Lace® Recipe		Traditional Recipe	
Calories	230	Calories	278
Calories from Fat	72	Calories from Fat	138
Total Fat	8 g	Total Fat	15 g
Cholesterol	25 mg	Cholesterol	48 mg

Buffet bound—two perfect vegetables drizzled with a reduced fat Cheddar cheese sauce.

LOW FAT

CHEESE-STUFFED PEPPERS

6 small green, yellow or red bell peppers

2 cups canned crushed tomatoes, undrained

⅓ cup water

⅓ cup slivered fresh basil leaves

1 tablespoon vegetable oil

1 cup chopped yellow onion

2 teaspoons minced garlic

2 cups cooked long grain white rice

½ cup minced fresh parsley

1½ teaspoons dried marjoram

¼ teaspoon salt

⅛ teaspoon red pepper flakes

1 cup (4 ounces) shredded Alpine Lace® Reduced Fat Swiss Cheese

1 To parboil the peppers: Half-fill a large saucepan with cold water and bring to a boil over high heat. Using a small pointed knife, trim the top ½ inch off of the peppers and remove the seeds and ribs. To enable the peppers to stand up straight, trim about ¼ inch off of the bottoms, being careful not to cut through the bottoms. Simmer the peppers in the water, uncovered, for 2 to 3 minutes, then remove with tongs or a slotted spoon and drain.

2 To make the sauce: In a medium-size saucepan, bring the tomatoes, water and basil to a boil over medium-high heat. Set aside.

3 Preheat the oven to 350°F. Spray an 8-inch round baking dish with nonstick cooking spray.

4 To make the stuffing: In a small nonstick skillet, heat the oil over medium-high heat. Add the onion and garlic and sauté for 5 minutes or until soft. Remove the skillet from the heat. Stir in the rice, half of the tomato sauce, the parsley, marjoram, salt, red pepper flakes and cheese.

5 Stuff the rice mixture into the peppers, then stand them upright in the baking dish. Bake, uncovered, for 30 minutes. Top the peppers with the remaining tomato sauce and continue baking 10 minutes more or until the peppers are tender and the sauce is bubbly. Serve hot! *Makes 6 servings*

Nutritional Comparison Per Serving

Alpine Lace® Recipe		Traditional Recipe	
Calories	203	Calories	214
Calories from Fat	60	Calories from Fat	71
Total Fat	6 g	Total Fat	8 g
Cholesterol	13 mg	Cholesterol	17 mg

Bell peppers stuffed with reduced fat Swiss cheese—a marvelous meatless dish.

LOW FAT

ROSY POTATO AND PEPPER GRATIN

3 tablespoons extra virgin
  olive oil
1 tablespoon fresh thyme leaves
  or 1 teaspoon dried thyme
½ teaspoon salt
½ teaspoon freshly ground black
  pepper
3 pounds unpeeled red-skinned
  potatoes, sliced ¼ inch
  thick (4 cups)
2 cups thin strips yellow onion
2 cups thin strips red bell
  pepper

3 cups (12 ounces) shredded
  Alpine Lace® Fat Free
  Pasteurized Process Skim
  Milk Cheese Product—
  For Mozzarella Lovers
¼ cup low sodium chicken broth
¼ cup white wine or chicken
  broth
  Sprigs of fresh thyme
  (optional)

1 Preheat the oven to 375°F. Spray a 13 × 9 × 3-inch baking dish with nonstick cooking spray. In a cup, mix the oil, thyme, salt and black pepper.

2 Half-fill a large saucepan with water and bring to a boil over high heat. Add the potatoes, cover, remove from the heat and let stand for 10 minutes. Drain the potatoes well and transfer them to a large bowl. Drizzle with the oil mixture.

3 Line the bottom of the baking dish with a third of the potatoes. Layer with half of the onions, half of the bell pepper strips and a third of the cheese. Repeat layers beginning with the potatoes, then top with the remaining third of the potatoes and cheese.

4 In a measuring cup, combine the chicken broth and wine. Pour evenly over the gratin. Cover with foil and bake for 20 minutes. Remove the foil and bake for 30 minutes or until the potatoes are tender and the top is golden brown. Garnish with the thyme sprigs, if you wish.

Makes 8 servings

Nutritional Comparison Per Serving

Alpine Lace® Recipe		Traditional Recipe	
Calories	289	Calories	341
Calories from Fat	48	Calories from Fat	130
Total Fat	5 g	Total Fat	15 g
Cholesterol	5 mg	Cholesterol	33 mg

A low fat version of potatoes au gratin—layered with red-skinned potatoes, strips of red bell pepper and fat free mozzarella.

Best for Brunch!

*Even egg dishes get a great start with Alpine Lace®
cheeses. Whip up a Swiss soufflé, whisk up a frittata,
bake up a quiche or layer up a bread pudding.
Then serve them up with the satisfaction that you've
trimmed back the fat!*

REDUCED FAT

20% less fat than the traditional recipe

SAVORY BREAD PUDDING

8 slices thick-cut, day-old white
    bread, crusts trimmed
2 tablespoons unsalted butter
    substitute, softened
2 cups (8 ounces) shredded
    Alpine Lace® Reduced Fat
    Swiss Cheese, divided
1 cup grated peeled apple

½ cup egg substitute or
    2 large eggs
2 large egg whites
2 cups 2% low fat milk
½ teaspoon salt
¼ teaspoon freshly ground black
    pepper

1 Preheat the oven to 400°F. Spray a 13×9×2-inch rectangular or 3-quart oval baking dish with nonstick cooking spray. Thinly spread the bread slices with the butter. Cut each bread slice into 4 triangles, making a total of 32. In a small bowl, toss 1¾ cups of the cheese with the grated apple.

2 In a medium-size bowl, using an electric mixer set on high, beat the egg substitute (or the whole eggs), the egg whites, milk, salt and pepper together until frothy and light yellow.

3 To assemble the pudding: Line the bottom of the dish with 16 of the bread triangles. Cover with the apple-cheese mixture, then pour over half the egg mixture. Arrange the remaining 16 triangles around the edge and down the center of the dish, overlapping slightly as you go.

continued on page 70

A pudding that's not for dessert, but for brunch!

4 Pour the remaining egg mixture over the top, then sprinkle with the remaining ¼ cup of cheese. Bake, uncovered, for 35 minutes or until crisp and golden brown.

Makes 8 servings

Nutritional Comparison Per Serving

Alpine Lace® Recipe		Traditional Recipe	
Calories	254	Calories	279
Calories from Fat	107	Calories from Fat	135
Total Fat	12 g	Total Fat	15 g
Cholesterol	33 mg	Cholesterol	96 mg

REDUCED FAT

64% less fat than the traditional recipe

EGGS BENEDICT MOUSSELINE

6 ounces (1 carton) Alpine Lace® Fat Free Cream Cheese with Garden Vegetables
¼ cup 2% low fat milk
1 tablespoon unsalted butter substitute
1 tablespoon fresh lemon juice

Dash cayenne pepper
2 regular-size English muffins, split
4 thin slices (½ ounce each) Alpine Lace® Boneless Cooked Ham, divided
1 teaspoon white vinegar
4 large eggs

1 Preheat the broiler. In a medium-size saucepan, heat the cheese, milk and butter over medium heat until the cheese is melted, then whisk in the lemon juice and pepper. Keep warm.

2 On a baking sheet, arrange the 4 muffin halves, split sides up. Broil for 1 minute or until golden brown; keep warm. In a large nonstick skillet, cook the ham over medium heat for 2 minutes. Place one slice of ham on each muffin half. Wipe out the skillet.

3 Fill the skillet two-thirds full with water. Add the vinegar and bring to a simmer over medium heat. Break each egg into a saucer, then slide it into the water. Spoon the water gently over the eggs for 3 minutes or until they are the way you like them. Using a slotted spoon, place 1 egg on each muffin, ladle some sauce over the top and serve.

Makes 4 servings

Nutritional Comparison Per Serving
(1 egg + ½ muffin)

Alpine Lace® Recipe		Traditional Recipe	
Calories	234	Calories	354
Calories from Fat	79	Calories from Fat	225
Total Fat	9 g	Total Fat	25 g
Cholesterol	228 mg	Cholesterol	279 mg

REDUCED FAT

42% less fat than the traditional recipe

GARDEN FRITTATA

1 tablespoon extra virgin
 olive oil
1 cup sliced, unpeeled, small
 red-skinned potatoes
 (about 4 ounces)
½ cup chopped red onion
½ cup chopped red bell pepper
1 teaspoon minced garlic
1 cup chopped fresh asparagus
½ cup fresh corn kernels or
 frozen corn, thawed and
 drained
1 cup diced Alpine Lace®
 Boneless Cooked Ham
 (4 ounces)

¾ cup egg substitute or 3 large
 eggs
3 large egg whites
1 cup (4 ounces) shredded
 Alpine Lace® Reduced Fat
 Lightly Smoked Provolone
 Cheese
¼ cup slivered fresh basil leaves
 or 1 tablespoon dried basil
½ teaspoon salt
¼ teaspoon freshly ground black
 pepper

1 Preheat the broiler. In a large broilerproof nonstick skillet, heat the oil over medium-high heat. Add the potatoes, onion, bell pepper and garlic. Cook, stirring occasionally, for 7 minutes or until the potatoes are almost tender. Stir in the asparagus, corn and ham and cook 3 minutes more or until the vegetables are crisp-tender.

2 In a medium-size bowl, whisk the egg substitute (or the whole eggs), the egg whites, cheese, basil, salt and black pepper together until blended. Pour over the vegetables. Reduce the heat and cook, uncovered, for 8 minutes or just until the egg mixture is set around the edges.

3 Slide the skillet under the broiler for 1 minute or until the eggs are set in the center. Serve immediately.   *Makes 4 servings*

Nutritional Comparison Per Serving

Alpine Lace® Recipe		Traditional Recipe	
Calories	250	Calories	335
Calories from Fat	99	Calories from Fat	168
Total Fat	11 g	Total Fat	19 g
Cholesterol	28 mg	Cholesterol	250 mg

REDUCED FAT

36% less fat than the traditional recipe

ASPARAGUS-SWISS SOUFFLÉ

¼ cup unsalted butter substitute
½ cup chopped yellow onion
¼ cup all-purpose flour
½ teaspoon salt
¼ teaspoon cayenne pepper
1 cup 2% low fat milk
1 cup (4 ounces) shredded Alpine Lace® Reduced Fat Swiss Cheese

1 cup egg substitute or 4 large eggs
1 cup coarsely chopped fresh asparagus pieces, cooked or frozen asparagus pieces, thawed and drained
3 large egg whites

1 Preheat the oven to 325°F. Spray a 1½-quart soufflé dish with nonstick cooking spray.

2 In a large saucepan, melt the butter over medium heat, add the onion and sauté for 5 minutes or until soft. Stir in the flour, salt and pepper and cook for 2 minutes or until bubbly. Add the milk and cook, stirring constantly, for 5 minutes or until the sauce thickens. Add the cheese and stir until melted.

3 In a small bowl, whisk the egg substitute (or the whole eggs). Whisk in a little of the hot cheese sauce, then return this egg mixture to the saucepan and whisk until well blended. Remove from the heat and fold in the drained asparagus.

4 In a medium-size bowl, using an electric mixer set on high, beat the egg whites until stiff peaks form. Fold the hot cheese sauce into the whites, then spoon into the soufflé dish.

5 Place the soufflé on a baking sheet and bake for 50 minutes or until golden brown and puffy.

Makes 8 servings

Nutritional Comparison Per Serving

Alpine Lace® Recipe		Traditional Recipe	
Calories	164	Calories	194
Calories from Fat	88	Calories from Fat	122
Total Fat	9 g	Total Fat	14 g
Cholesterol	13 mg	Cholesterol	140 mg

Welcome in Spring with this asparagus soufflé made the lower fat way.

LOW FAT

BROCCOLI & CHEESE QUICHE

2 cups zwieback crumbs
½ teaspoon ground nutmeg
⅓ cup honey
2 cups fresh broccoli florets or frozen broccoli florets, thawed and drained
½ tablespoon unsalted butter substitute
1 cup chopped yellow onion
1 cup (4 ounces) shredded Alpine Lace® Reduced Fat Swiss Cheese

1 cup (4 ounces) shredded Alpine Lace® Reduced Fat Colby Cheese
1 cup chopped red bell pepper
¾ cup egg substitute or 3 large eggs
2 large egg whites
¾ cup 2% low fat milk
½ teaspoon dry mustard
½ teaspoon salt
¼ teaspoon freshly ground white pepper

1 Preheat the oven to 400°F. Spray a 10-inch pie plate with nonstick cooking spray. To make the crumb crust: Toss the crumbs and nutmeg with the honey until the crumbs are thoroughly coated. Press onto the bottom and up the side of the pie plate.

2 To make the filling: Coarsely chop the broccoli. Half-fill a medium-size saucepan with water and bring to a boil over medium-high heat. Add the broccoli and cook, uncovered, for 5 minutes or just until crisp-tender. Drain.

3 In a small nonstick skillet, melt the butter over medium-high heat. Add the onion and sauté for 5 minutes or until soft. Layer both of the cheeses, then the onion, bell pepper and broccoli in the crust.

4 In a medium-size bowl, whisk the egg substitute (or the whole eggs), the egg whites, milk, mustard, salt and pepper together until blended. Pour evenly over the vegetables in the crust.

5 Bake for 10 minutes. Reduce the oven temperature to 350°F. Bake 20 minutes longer or until golden brown and puffy and a knife inserted in the center comes out clean.

Makes 8 servings

Nutritional Comparison Per Serving

Alpine Lace® Recipe		Traditional Recipe	
Calories	297	Calories	387
Calories from Fat	90	Calories from Fat	171
Total Fat	10 g	Total Fat	19 g
Cholesterol	27 mg	Cholesterol	130 mg

Whisk up a good-for-you quiche from broccoli and two reduced fat cheeses.

HOME-BAKED BREADS

Home-baked breads hot out of the oven—nothing tastes more delicious! Try Tex-Mex Corn Bread made with hot pepper cheese, Cheesy Buttermilk Biscuits made with shreds of Alpine Lace® Cheddar or Lemon Crème Tea Ring swirled with plenty of reduced sodium Muenster.

LOW FAT

APPLE CHEDDAR MUFFINS

2 cups sifted all-purpose flour
1 tablespoon baking powder
⅓ cup sugar
½ teaspoon salt
¼ teaspoon ground nutmeg
½ cup egg substitute or 2 large eggs
¾ cup 2% low fat milk
¼ cup unsalted butter, melted

1 cup grated, cored, peeled baking apples, such as Granny Smith, Rome Beauty or Winesap
¾ cup (3 ounces) shredded Alpine Lace® Fat Free Pasteurized Process Skim Milk Cheese Product— For Cheddar Lovers

1 Preheat the oven to 400°F. Spray 12 regular-size muffin cups with nonstick cooking spray.

2 In a large bowl, sift together the flour, baking powder, sugar, salt and nutmeg. In a small bowl, whisk the egg substitute (or the whole eggs) with the milk and butter until blended.

3 Using a wooden spoon, make a hole in the center of the flour mixture, then pour in the egg mixture all at once. Stir just until the flour disappears. *(Avoid overmixing!)* Fold in the apples and cheese. Spoon the batter into the muffin cups until three-fourths full.

continued on page 78

Hot homemade muffins, stirred up from fresh apples and fat free Cheddar.

4 Bake the muffins for 20 to 25 minutes or until golden brown. Cool the muffins in the pan on a wire rack for 5 minutes, then lift them out with a spatula. They're delicious when served hot with honey!   *Makes 12 muffins*

Nutritional Comparison Per Serving
(1 muffin)

Alpine Lace® Recipe		Traditional Recipe	
Calories	165	Calories	186
Calories from Fat	45	Calories from Fat	71
Total Fat	5 g	Total Fat	8 g
Cholesterol	13 mg	Cholesterol	56 mg

REDUCED FAT

22% less fat than the traditional recipe

CHEESY BUTTERMILK BISCUITS

2 cups all-purpose flour
1 tablespoon baking powder
1 teaspoon salt
½ teaspoon baking soda
½ teaspoon red pepper flakes
⅓ cup vegetable shortening

2 tablespoons unsalted butter, at room temperature
¾ cup low fat buttermilk
1 cup (4 ounces) shredded Alpine Lace® Reduced Fat Cheddar Cheese

1 Preheat the oven to 450°F. Spray a baking sheet with nonstick cooking spray. In a large bowl, stir together the flour, baking powder, salt, baking soda and red pepper flakes.

2 Using a pastry cutter or 2 knives, cut in the shortening and butter until coarse crumbs form. Using a wooden spoon, stir in the buttermilk and cheese just until a soft dough forms.

3 Turn the dough onto a lightly floured board and knead for about 30 seconds. Pat or roll the dough until it is 1 inch thick. Using a 2-inch biscuit cutter (preferably a fluted one), cut out 16 biscuits, re-rolling the scraps of dough as you go.

4 Place the biscuits 2 inches apart on the baking sheet and brush the tops with additional buttermilk, if you wish. Bake for 12 minutes or just until golden brown.   *Makes 16 biscuits*

Nutritional Comparison Per Serving
(1 biscuit)

Alpine Lace® Recipe		Traditional Recipe	
Calories	134	Calories	142
Calories from Fat	65	Calories from Fat	78
Total Fat	7 g	Total Fat	9 g
Cholesterol	8 mg	Cholesterol	12 mg

LOW FAT

PICK-OF-THE-GARDEN BREAD

3 cups all-purpose flour
1½ tablespoons baking powder
1 teaspoon salt
⅛ teaspoon cayenne pepper
6 tablespoons unsalted butter,
   at room temperature
6 ounces (1 carton) Alpine
   Lace® Fat Free Cream
   Cheese with Garden
   Vegetables

¾ cup 2% low fat milk
½ cup egg substitute or
   2 large eggs
¾ cup grated zucchini
½ cup grated peeled carrot
½ cup finely chopped green
   onions

1 Preheat the oven to 350°F. Spray a 9 × 5 × 3-inch loaf pan with nonstick cooking spray. In a large bowl, stir together the flour, baking powder, salt and pepper. Using a pastry blender or 2 knives, cut in the butter until coarse crumbs form.

2 In a small bowl, using an electric mixer set on medium, beat the cream cheese, milk and egg substitute (or the whole eggs) until almost blended.

3 Using a wooden spoon, make a hole in the center of the flour mixture and pour in the cheese mixture all at once. Stir just until the flour disappears. *(Avoid overmixing!)* Fold in the zucchini, carrot and green onions. Spoon the batter into the pan.

4 Bake for 1 hour and 20 minutes or until a toothpick inserted in the center comes out with moist crumbs. Cool the bread in the pan on a wire rack for 5 minutes, then remove from the pan to the rack to cool completely.

Makes one 9-inch loaf

Nutritional Comparison Per Serving
(¾-inch slice)

Alpine Lace® Recipe		Traditional Recipe	
Calories	207	Calories	246
Calories from Fat	63	Calories from Fat	114
Total Fat	7 g	Total Fat	13 g
Cholesterol	20 mg	Cholesterol	70 mg

LOW FAT

LEMON CRÈME TEA RING

1 pound frozen bread dough, thawed

3 tablespoons unsalted butter substitute, melted, divided

1 cup shredded Alpine Lace® Reduced Sodium Muenster Cheese

½ cup plus ¾ cup sifted confectioners' sugar

2 tablespoons 2% low fat milk

1 large egg yolk

1 teaspoon grated lemon rind

1½ teaspoons vanilla extract, divided

½ cup seedless golden raisins

2 tablespoons fresh lemon juice

1 Spray a 15 × 10-inch baking sheet with nonstick cooking spray.

2 To make the tea ring: On a lightly floured board, pat out the dough into a 16 × 12-inch rectangle and brush with 2 tablespoons of the butter.

3 In a food processor or blender, process the cheese, the ½ cup of sugar, the milk, egg yolk, lemon rind and 1 teaspoon vanilla for 15 seconds or just until blended. *(Avoid overprocessing!)* Spread the cheese mixture over the dough, leaving a ½-inch border, then sprinkle evenly with the raisins.

4 Starting at one of the narrow ends, roll up the dough jelly-roll style. Place on the baking sheet, seam side down, then form into a circle, pinching the ends together. Using scissors, cut at ½-inch intervals from the outside of the ring toward, but not through, the center. Slightly twist each section a half turn, allowing the filling to show. Cover and let rise for 1 hour or until doubled in size.

5 Preheat the oven to 375°F. Uncover the ring and brush the top with the remaining tablespoon of butter. Bake for 20 minutes or just until golden brown. Using a large spatula, carefully slide the tea ring onto a wire rack to cool for 15 minutes.

6 While the tea ring is cooling, make the icing: In a small bowl, beat the ¾ cup of sugar, the lemon juice and the remaining ½ teaspoon vanilla until smooth. Using a small spoon, drizzle the icing over the top of the warm tea ring.

Makes 14 servings

Nutritional Comparison Per Serving

Alpine Lace® Recipe		Traditional Recipe	
Calories	193	Calories	202
Calories from Fat	58	Calories from Fat	66
Total Fat	6 g	Total Fat	8 g
Cholesterol	30 mg	Cholesterol	31 mg

A gem of a tea ring—divine as a coffeecake and delicious for dessert!

38% less fat than the traditional recipe

CHEDDAR AND ONION WHOLE WHEAT LOAF

½ cup egg substitute or
    2 large eggs
⅔ cup 2% low fat milk
1⅓ cups whole wheat flour
    1 cup all-purpose flour
1½ tablespoons baking powder
¾ teaspoon salt
½ teaspoon coarsely ground
    black pepper

3 tablespoons unsalted butter,
    at room temperature
1 cup (4 ounces) shredded
    Alpine Lace® Reduced Fat
    Cheddar Cheese
1 cup minced yellow onion

1 Preheat the oven to 350°F. Spray a 9 × 5 × 3-inch loaf pan with nonstick cooking spray. In a cup, whisk the egg substitute (or the whole eggs) with the milk. In a large bowl, stir together both of the flours, the baking powder, salt and pepper. Using a pastry blender or 2 knives, cut in the butter until coarse crumbs form.

2 Using a wooden spoon, make a hole in the center of the flour mixture, then pour in the egg mixture all at once. Stir just until the flour disappears. *(Avoid overmixing!)* Fold in the cheese and onion, then spoon the batter into the pan.

3 Bake the bread for 1 hour and 10 minutes or until a toothpick inserted in the center comes out with moist crumbs. Cool the bread in the pan on a wire rack for 5 minutes, then remove from the pan to the rack to cool completely.

Makes one 9-inch loaf

Nutritional Comparison Per Serving
(¾-inch slice)

Alpine Lace® Recipe		Traditional Recipe	
Calories	160	Calories	175
Calories from Fat	50	Calories from Fat	68
Total Fat	5 g	Total Fat	8 g
Cholesterol	14 mg	Cholesterol	55 mg

Healthy, hearty and homemade—a whole wheat bread flavored with plenty of reduced fat Cheddar, onion and black pepper.

LOW FAT

TEX-MEX CORN BREAD

1½ cups all-purpose flour
¾ cup yellow cornmeal
2 tablespoons sugar
1 tablespoon baking powder
1 teaspoon baking soda
¾ teaspoon salt
1⅓ cups low fat buttermilk
3 tablespoons unsalted butter, melted
½ cup finely chopped red bell pepper

¼ cup minced green onions
1 cup fresh corn kernels or frozen corn, thawed
¾ cup (3 ounces) shredded Alpine Lace® American Flavor Pasteurized Process Cheese Product with Jalapeño Peppers

1 Preheat the oven to 425°F. Spray a deep ovenproof 10-inch skillet (preferably cast iron) with nonstick cooking spray and place in the oven on the middle rack to heat.

2 In a large bowl, stir together the flour, cornmeal, sugar, baking powder, baking soda and salt. In a medium-size bowl, whisk together the buttermilk and butter. Stir in the bell pepper and green onions.

3 Using a wooden spoon, make a hole in the center of the flour mixture, then pour in the buttermilk mixture all at once. Stir just until the flour disappears. *(Avoid overmixing!)* Fold in the corn and cheese. Spoon the batter into the hot skillet.

4 Bake the bread for 25 minutes or until golden brown and a toothpick inserted in the center comes out with moist crumbs. Serve immediately, straight from the skillet.

Makes 12 servings

Nutritional Comparison Per Serving

Alpine Lace® Recipe		Traditional Recipe	
Calories	164	Calories	170
Calories from Fat	47	Calories from Fat	53
Total Fat	5 g	Total Fat	6 g
Cholesterol	14 mg	Cholesterol	16 mg

A south-of-the-border treat—corn bread straight from the old iron skillet is spiced just right with reduced fat jalapeño peppered cheese.

SWEET ENDINGS

> *Surprise! When you start with Alpine Lace® cheese, you can even make sweets slimmer than usual!*

REDUCED FAT

38% less fat than the traditional recipe

APPLE STRUDEL

1 sheet (½ of a 17¼-ounce package) frozen puff pastry
1 cup (4 ounces) shredded Alpine Lace® Reduced Fat Cheddar Cheese
2 large Granny Smith apples, peeled, cored and sliced ⅛ inch thick (12 ounces)

⅓ cup golden raisins
2 tablespoons apple brandy (optional)
¼ cup granulated sugar
¼ cup packed light brown sugar
½ teaspoon ground cinnamon
2 tablespoons unsalted butter substitute, melted

1 To shape the pastry: Thaw the pastry for 20 minutes. Preheat the oven to 350°F. On a floured board, roll the pastry into a 15 × 12-inch rectangle.

2 To make the filling: Sprinkle the cheese on the dough, leaving a 1-inch border. Arrange the apples on top. Sprinkle with the raisins, then the brandy, if you wish. In a small cup, mix both of the sugars with the cinnamon, then sprinkle over the apple filling.

3 Starting from one of the wide ends, roll up jelly-roll style. Place on a baking sheet, seam side down, tucking the ends under. Using a sharp knife, make 7 diagonal slits on the top, then brush with the butter. Bake for 35 minutes or until golden brown.   *Makes 18 servings*

Nutritional Comparison Per Serving

Alpine Lace® Recipe		Traditional Recipe	
Calories	151	Calories	197
Calories from Fat	75	Calories from Fat	113
Total Fat	8 g	Total Fat	13 g
Cholesterol	6 mg	Cholesterol	34 mg

Easy strudel from apples, frozen pastry and reduced fat Cheddar.

REDUCED FAT

31% less fat than the traditional recipe

THREE-BERRY TART

2 cups all-purpose flour
5 tablespoons unsalted butter
¼ cup ground almonds
⅓ cup plus ½ cup sifted
    confectioners' sugar
5 tablespoons ice water
1 tablespoon cornstarch
⅓ cup 2% low fat milk
1 cup (4 ounces) shredded
    Alpine Lace® Reduced
    Sodium Muenster Cheese

1½ cups low fat sour cream
1 cup vanilla nonfat yogurt
1 tablespoon vanilla extract
1 teaspoon grated lemon rind
2 cups strawberries, hulled and
    halved
1½ cups fresh raspberries
1½ cups fresh blueberries
1 cup peeled kiwi slices
½ cup red currant jelly

1 To make the almond crust: Preheat the oven to 400°F. In a medium-size bowl, mix the flour, butter, almonds and the ⅓ cup of confectioners' sugar with your fingers until coarse crumbs form. Add enough water to form a dough. Press onto the bottom and up the side of a 12-inch tart pan with a removable bottom. Prick the dough at ½-inch intervals with the tines of a fork and bake for 15 minutes or until golden brown.

2 Meanwhile, make the cheese filling: In a small saucepan, dissolve the cornstarch in the milk. Stir in the cheese and cook over medium heat until the mixture is slightly thickened and smooth. Cool for 15 minutes.

3 In a medium-size bowl, with an electric mixer set on medium-high, beat the sour cream, yogurt, the ½ cup of confectioners' sugar, the vanilla and lemon rind for 1 minute. With the mixer running, slowly add the cheese mixture and beat until the filling is almost smooth. Pour into the tart shell and refrigerate for 30 minutes or until filling is thickened and cold.

4 To make the fresh fruit topping: Arrange the berries and kiwi slices decoratively on top of the filling. In a small saucepan, melt the jelly over low heat, then carefully brush over the berries and kiwi. Refrigerate for at least 1 hour before serving.

Makes 16 servings

Nutritional Comparison Per Serving

Alpine Lace® Recipe		Traditional Recipe	
Calories	240	Calories	267
Calories from Fat	77	Calories from Fat	115
Total Fat	9 g	Total Fat	13 g
Cholesterol	21 mg	Cholesterol	30 mg

Party-perfect tart with fresh fruits swirled on a Muenster crème.

REDUCED FAT

25% less fat than the traditional recipe

LEMON CRÈME BARS

CRUST

2 cups sifted all-purpose flour

¾ cup sifted confectioners' sugar

1 teaspoon grated lemon rind

½ cup unsalted butter, at room temperature

2 tablespoons cold water

LEMON FILLING

½ cup egg substitute or 2 large eggs

1¾ cups granulated sugar

¾ cup (3 ounces) shredded Alpine Lace® Reduced Sodium Muenster Cheese

1½ cups sifted all-purpose flour

1 tablespoon baking powder

⅔ cup fresh lemon juice

1 teaspoon grated lemon rind

¼ cup slivered almonds (optional)

3 tablespoons sifted confectioners' sugar

Additional grated lemon rind (optional)

1 To make the Crust: Preheat the oven to 350°F and butter a 13 × 9 × 2-inch baking pan. In a medium-size bowl, mix the flour, confectioners' sugar and lemon rind, then work in the butter with your fingers until coarse crumbs form. Add the water and continue mixing until a dough forms. Press evenly onto the bottom of the baking pan and bake for 10 minutes.

2 While the crust is baking, make the Lemon Filling: In a medium-size bowl, whisk the egg substitute (or the whole eggs) until light yellow. Whisk in the granulated sugar, cheese, flour, baking powder, lemon juice and lemon rind until well blended. Pour the egg mixture over the hot crust and sprinkle with the almonds, if you wish. Return to the oven and bake 25 minutes longer or until the filling is set.

3 Cool the cookies in the pan on a wire rack for 10 minutes, then cut into 36 (2 × 1½-inch) bars. Cool on wire racks. Dust with the confectioners' sugar. Garnish with additional lemon rind, if you wish. Refrigerate in an airtight container.

Makes 3 dozen bars

Nutritional Comparison Per Serving
(1 bar)

Alpine Lace® Recipe		Traditional Recipe	
Calories	105	Calories	128
Calories from Fat	33	Calories from Fat	36
Total Fat	3 g	Total Fat	4 g
Cholesterol	9 mg	Cholesterol	21 mg

A heavenly lemon dessert bar—cuts like a cookie, eats like a creamy pie.

REDUCED FAT

27% less fat than the traditional recipe

NAPOLEONS

1 sheet (½ of a 17¼-ounce
    package) frozen puff pastry
1½ cups (6 ounces) shredded
    Alpine Lace® Reduced
    Sodium Muenster Cheese
¼ cup 2% low fat milk
2 cups low fat sour cream
½ cup plus ¼ cup sifted
    confectioners' sugar

2 teaspoons vanilla extract
1 teaspoon grated lemon rind
3 ounces semi-sweet chocolate,
    melted
1 tablespoon unsalted butter
    substitute

1 To prepare the puff pastry: Thaw the pastry for 20 minutes. Preheat the oven to 400°F. On a lightly floured board, roll out the pastry into a 12 × 10-inch rectangle. Using a sharp pointed knife, cut into 20 (3 × 2-inch) strips. Bake for 12 minutes or until golden brown and puffy. Transfer to a wire rack to cool.

2 Meanwhile, make the crème filling: In a small saucepan, heat the cheese and milk over medium heat until the cheese is melted and the mixture is smooth. Cool for 15 minutes.

3 In a medium-size bowl, with an electric mixer set on medium-high, beat the sour cream, ½ cup of sugar, vanilla and lemon rind for 1 minute. With the mixer running, slowly add the cheese mixture and beat until almost smooth. Refrigerate for 1 hour or until thickened and cold.

4 To assemble the Napoleons: Using a serrated knife, split each pastry rectangle horizontally into 2 equal pieces, then fill with about 3 tablespoons of the filling.

5 To make the topping: Sprinkle the top of each Napoleon with a little of the ¼ cup of sugar. In a small saucepan, melt the chocolate with the butter, stirring until blended. Drizzle immediately on top of each pastry.

Makes 20 Napoleons

Nutritional Comparison Per Serving
(1 Napoleon)

Alpine Lace® Recipe		Traditional Recipe	
Calories	169	Calories	202
Calories from Fat	97	Calories from Fat	135
Total Fat	11 g	Total Fat	15 g
Cholesterol	13 mg	Cholesterol	22 mg

TRIM THE FAT

Choose Alpine Lace® cheeses—you get excellent flavor
and great nutritional benefits. Look and compare!

Reduced Fat/Reduced Sodium Cheeses (Serving Size: 1 ounce)

Type of Cheese	Calories	Fat	Cholesterol
Alpine Lace® American Flavor Pasteurized Process Cheese Product (or with Jalapeño Peppers)	80	6 g	20 mg
Regular American	110	9 g	25 mg
Alpine Lace® Reduced Fat Swiss	90	6 g	20 mg
Regular Swiss	110	8 g	25 mg
Alpine Lace® Reduced Fat Cheddar	80	4.5 g	15 mg
Regular Cheddar	110	9 g	30 mg
Alpine Lace® Reduced Sodium Low Moisture Part-Skim Mozzarella	70	5 g	15 mg
Regular Low Moisture Part-Skim Mozzarella	80	5 g	15 mg
Alpine Lace® Reduced Fat Provolone	70	5 g	15 mg
Regular Provolone	100	8 g	20 mg
Alpine Lace® Reduced Fat Colby	80	5 g	15 mg
Regular Colby	110	9 g	25 mg

Fat Free Cheese Products (Serving Size: 1 ounce)

Type of Cheese	Calories	Fat	Cholesterol
Alpine Lace® Fat Free Cream Cheese with Garlic & Herbs or Garden Vegetables	40	0 g	<5 mg
Regular Cream Cheese	100	10 g	30 mg
Alpine Lace® Fat Free Cheese Spread— Mexican Nacho	40	0 g	<5 mg
Regular Cheddar	110	9 g	30 mg
Alpine Lace® Fat Free American Flavor	45	0 g	<5 mg
Regular American	110	9 g	25 mg
Alpine Lace® Fat Free Cheddar Flavor	45	0 g	<5 mg
Regular Cheddar	110	9 g	30 mg
Alpine Lace® Fat Free Mozzarella Flavor	45	0 g	<5 mg
Regular Whole Milk Mozzarella	80	6 g	20 mg
Alpine Lace® Fat Free Parmesan Flavor	60	0 g	<5 mg
Regular Parmesan	130	9 g	20 mg